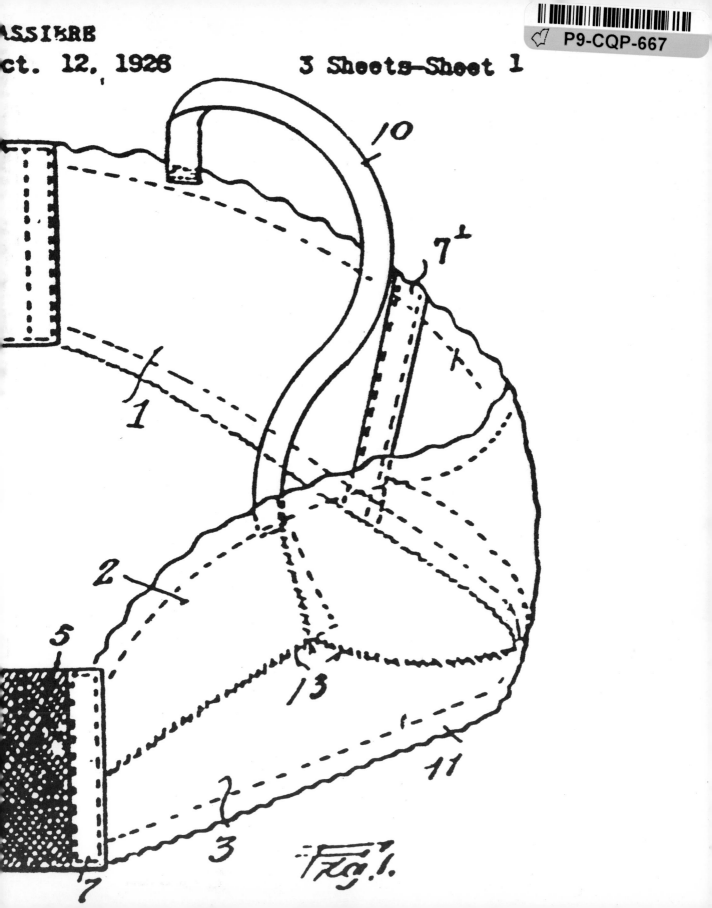

Fig.1.

UN-
MENTIONABLES

A BRIEF HISTORY OF UNDERWEAR UN-MENTIONABLES

ELAINE BENSON

JOHN ESTEN

SIMON & SCHUSTER EDITIONS

Published by Simon & Schuster

END PAPERS:
Schematic drawing (Sheets 1 and 2) of patent application for the
William Rosenthal brassiere, filed October 12, 1926.
The Maidenform Museum, New York City. William Rosenthal
was president and chief designer of the Maidenform Brassiere
Company. The application states that the novel design of this
garment "support[s] the bust in a natural position, contrary to
the old idea of brassieres made to flatten down the bust . . ."

OPPOSITE TITLE PAGE:
Carlo Mollino (1905–1973), Italian. Retouched Polaroid,
between 1953 and 1968. ©1968, Carlo Mollino. Courtesy
Robert Miller Gallery, New York City. The architect-designer's
hobby was photographing women, often dressed in lingerie,
in provocative poses.

SIMON & SCHUSTER EDITIONS
ROCKEFELLER CENTER
1230 AVENUE OF THE AMERICAS
NEW YORK, NY 10020

DESIGNED BY JOHN ESTEN

PRINTED IN ITALY

1   3   5   7   9   10   8   6   4   2

LIBRARY OF CONGRESS CATALOGING-IN-PUBLICATION DATA
Benson, Elaine.
Unmentionables, a brief history of underwear / Elaine Benson with John Esten.
p.   cm.
Includes bibliographical references.
1. Underwear—History. 2. Underwear—Social aspects. I. Esten, John, date.
GT2073.B45   1996
391'.42'09—dc20   96-28663
                                    CIP

1SBN 0-684-82266-0

CREDITS APPEAR ON PAGE 159.

CONTENTS

ACKNOWLEDGMENTS

I wish to thank all of those who through the years have offered assistance, insights, clippings, and encouragement to this book project. Without their help it would not have been possible to complete it: Josepha A. Stewart, for her early collaboration in concept and research; Robert Heilbroner, an unexpected and splendid volunteer editor; my daughters, Virginia Goff Green and Kimberly Goff Knollenberg, for being there when I needed them; my sons, Neal and Bill Goff, for their support and advice; my husband, Joseph F. X. Kaufman, for his consistent involvement, French translations, and historical perspective; our agent, John Thornton, a good editor and friend; Jackie Seow; Peter McCulloch; Robin Zarensky, our editor at Simon & Schuster, for her commitment to this project; Betsy Goff, my smart contract-lawyer daughter-in-law, and, most especially, my thanks to John Esten. There are others who deserve to be mentioned: William Rossa Cole, Frances Ann and Frazer Dougherty, Claude Delibes, Danielle Hauss, Eleanor Lambert, the late Diana Vreeland, Jack Lenor Larsen, Nancy Love, the late John Maass; Eleanor Friede, Joy R. Kluess, Priscilla Bowden Potter, John Morris; Sugar Blum, Brent and Missy Lynch, Clare McLean, Jane Whitney, Arnold Scaasi, Parker Ladd, Sherrye Henry, Bonnie Cashin, Robert Riley, Martha Sheehan, Betty Smith, Mallory Hart, Catherine Brawer, and Gladys Walker; all of whom contributed either information or inspiration, or both, that was both welcome and needed.

John Esten wishes to thank and acknowledge the following people for their contributions: Catherine Bindman, Louis Botto, Jack Bringmann, Russell Bush, Cynthia Cathcart, Judith Calamandrei, P. J. Carlino, Jeanette Chang, Stephanie Clopton, Debra Cohen, Mary Doherty, Mary Doerhoefer, Diana Edkins, Reagan Fletcher, Sharon Frost, Robert Gable, Mona Gertner, Joshua Greene, Scott Hyde, Marty Jacobs, David Joseph, Robert Kaufmann, Howard Mandelbaum, Ron Mandelbaum, Annelies Mondi, Sarah Morthland, Brandusa Niro, Louisa Orto, Joan LiPuma, Howard Read, Walt Reed, Diana Reeve, Yvette Reyes, Alexandra Rowley, Beth Savage, Jessica Scarlata, Max Scheler, Natasha Sigmund, Anne Stegemeyer, Ali Taekman, Barbara Slifka, Christina Strassfield, Lucy White, Taki Wise, and Stephen Wood.

THE MONTH OF FEBRUARY. Detail of miniature from *Très Riches Heures du Duc de Berry*, 1411–16, Franco-Flemish. Musée Condé, Chantilly. Warming themselves by the fire, the peasants can be seen to wear nothing at all under their skirts and tunics.

PREFACE

It's not always easy to pin down the first stirrings of a love affair, but I know exactly when and where I became enamored of underwear, or at least with its history. The time was the early 1960s, and I was working as Coordinator of the Fashion Department of the Philadelphia Museum College of Art. (That's also when I first met John Esten, then a student at the art school.) I was a member of an organization of women fashion executives with a particular interest in the Fashion Wing of the Philadelphia Museum of Art, then affiliated with the art school. Our holdings were rich in gowns by Paul Poiret, Charles Worth, Madame Vionnet, Fortuny, and more contemporary couturiers, which were displayed in changing shows. The main draw, to be sure, was Grace Kelly's wedding gown (it seemed that when she married Prince Rainier of Monaco half of Philadelphia went to the wedding).

Behind the glamour of the display cases at the museum were "the stacks," drawer after drawer of shoes, fans, gloves, and to me most impressive of all, exquisitely made undergarments—handmade wisps of silk, lace, and embroidery, multiboned corsets, richly embellished petticoats—hinting at untold stories of the privileged, proper Philadelphians who had given them to the museum. These treasures were seen only by the professionals allowed in the storeroom for research; underwear was still considered too "unmentionable" to be shown to the public. I decided to write a book about it.

In the intervening years I filled boxes with clippings and notes, visited museum costume collections in Barcelona, Lisbon, Athens, and Paris, and haunted libraries. I found a few books about bras and knickers and corsets, catalogs of museum exhibitions, some French and English and German studies, but curiously, not much from the United States, although our country has led the world in producing underwear. Indeed, with all the attention paid to costume over the ages, very little has been written about the things that go underneath.

A short fling as a fashion writer at the *Philadelphia Inquirer* and thirty years running my own art gallery, then it all came together; I was finally ready to write the book. That's when I once again encountered John Esten, whose *Hampton Style: Houses, Gardens and Artists* had just been published. I infected John with my enthusiasm and, happily, he agreed to join the project as designer and art director; it is he who has searched out and selected the illustrations and designed this book.

The subject of underwear can still evoke smirks and titters but it arouses a kind of sociological fervor in me, for whom its history sheds light on women's long battle to attain freedom and social equality. I hope to show that it gives insight into our past and perspective to our present—and that underwear is not only "mentionable," it's fascinating. ∎

E.B.
Bridgehampton, New York

Structured bra, sheer petticoat. 1958. Photograph by Jerry Schatzberg, American, for *Vogue* magazine. Courtesy Staley-Wise Gallery, New York City. Ten years after the New Look, a pointed bra gives definition for fitted bodices, while sheer petticoats are layered to buoy full-circle skirts.

1

IN THE BEGINNING

And the eyes of them both were opened,
and they knew that they were naked;
and they sewed fig leaves together,
and made themselves aprons.

Genesis 3:7

Was an apron of fig leaves the first underwear? Underwear's antecedents are hard to track down—a sculpture or wall painting here, a painted vase or other archeological find there, some fragments of writing—bit by bit we assemble information and make deductions. We can see what was worn on the outside but only speculate about what the ancients wore under their tunics and robes, and it's hard to determine when the idea began of clothes meant specifically as underclothes.

From Egypt to Greece to Rome, one rule cut across cultures: the higher you stood on the social scale, the more you wore; slaves and peasants wore rudimentary coverings and, in Egypt at least, often nothing at all. Statuettes and wall paintings from ancient Egypt show female slaves in scanty *caches-sexe* much like a stripteaser's G-string, while in the Louvre, a bronze sculpture from Greece dated 3000 B.C., probably of a female slave, wears only a necklace and what look like bikini briefs. Today the situation is reversed: waiters, chauffeurs, and the like are often more formally dressed than those they serve.

When in search of underwear, there's a tendency to see it everywhere. From boxer shorts to briefs, to corsets and girdles, to waist cinchers and garter belts and brassieres—once you start looking for them they turn up in the most unlikely places. Such as in the Tyrolean Alps, where in 1991 mountaineers stumbled on the frozen body of a man thought to have lived up to fifty-three hundred years ago. Bits of clothing recovered with the body included fairly well-preserved animal skin leggings and a leather loincloth. The leggings were worn fur-side out and had sewn-in straps that hitched them to a body belt, under which the end of the loincloth was inserted. I consider this the earliest known garter belt. The loincloth itself is the universal antecedent of men's underwear. In 1352 B.C. Egypt, the young Pharaoh Tutankhamen was buried with 145 of them, which would seem to be an ample supply for the afterlife; over three thousand years later Japanese prisoners during World War II wore something similar under their uniforms.

Waist cinchers and corselettes? Look back to 2000 B.C. in Minoan Crete, where both men and women had extremely small waists, presumably from wearing a constricting belt or girdle from childhood. Men wore what was essentially a tightly belted loincloth, while women are shown in a

ADAM & EVE, 1526, oil on canvas.
Lucas Cranach the Elder (1472–1553), German.
Courtauld Institute Galleries, the Lee Collection,
London. Here strategically placed fig leaves are not
so much underwear as only wear.

severely nipped-in bodice ending below exposed breasts, plus a skirt that descends to the ground in a series of flounces and looks very much like a petticoat. The Ashmolean Museum in Oxford, England, owns a cast of a *ca.* 1700 B.C. Minoan sculpture of a Minoan priestess dressed this way. Perhaps she was the inspiration for Jean Paul Gaultier when he created Madonna's corset costume with its exaggerated cone-shaped cups?

The brassiere as we know it was not invented till the twentieth century, but we are told that women in ancient Greece strapped lengths of cloth or leather across their breasts under their chitons. From even earlier, a solid gold breastplate resembling a bra covered the breasts of female remains that were discovered in Lefkandi, Greece, and thought to date from 1000 B.C.

Nudity, at least for athletes and in art, was considered normal by the ancient Greeks, and the nude has been honored in art through the ages. But it is only in the late nineteenth century that artists were to show women or men in semiundress. Then, the women portrayed were generally prostitutes or models; when men were stripping down it was to go swimming.

Underwear has been associated with modesty or with the lack of it. But ideas of modesty vary with climates and cultures. Arabs are covered head to toe but wear no undergarments. Samoans consider it immodest to expose the navel. And Western influences, from missionaries to the movies, have everywhere altered local attitudes. In contemporary Bali you'll find older women working on construction sites, their breasts bared, while younger women wear bras under T-shirts imprinted with slogans. And in New Guinea, where missionaries' teachings have prevailed, women cover their inti-mate body parts with cloth. Elsewhere they wear grasses, creatively arranged but leaving their breasts exposed, and men wear only penis sheaths made of gourds held on by raffia ties.

Vestiges of missionary thinking can be found in unlikely places. Consider Southampton, New York, which found it necessary to promulgate a dress code, still in force: "No person shall appear in a public street of said village clothed or costumed in such a manner that the portion of his or her breast below the areola is not covered with fully opaque clothing. No person shall appear in a public street in said village unless his or her buttocks and the private and intimate parts of his or her body are covered with fully opaque covering." A violation can lead to a fine or even imprisonment.

The Victorians, despite the fact that they wore more of them than anyone before or since, called undergarments "unmentionables," and some diehards still feel that way. Airing one's linen in public is a metaphor for revealing private matters better kept under wraps, and there is a tendency to refer to underwear in a form of baby talk: undies, panties, scanties, snuggies, teddys, the manly skivvies, or the English smalls.

Inextricably associated with modesty and morality, status and sexuality, cleanliness and, sometimes, even Godliness, underwear becomes a complex subject, further complicated by fashion. Designer Arnold Scaasi is not alone when he says, "I am ever mindful of underpinnings. I like to think that I work as a sculptor does, using the body as an armature to be embellished." But since people dress neither logically, consistently, nor predictably, it's hardly surprising that what they wear next to their skin is full of contradictions. ∎

Snake Goddess from the Palace of Knossos, Crete, *ca.* 1700 B.C.
Cast of figurine in the Heraklion Museum, Crete.
Ashmolean Museum, Oxford, England.
The goddess wears what is considered the earliest version
of the corset and the antecedent of the petticoat.

Taking it off. *Above,* PARIS, LE SPHYNXE, 1956.
Frank Horvat, French. Courtesy Staley-Wise Gallery,
New York City. The G-string—underwear
in its sparest form.

Opposite, NEW YORK, 1953. Weegee (Arthur Felig,
1899–1968), American. Courtesy of Janet Lehr, Inc.,
New York City. Exotic dancer and jazz musicians
shown with the gritty realism for which the
photographer was noted.

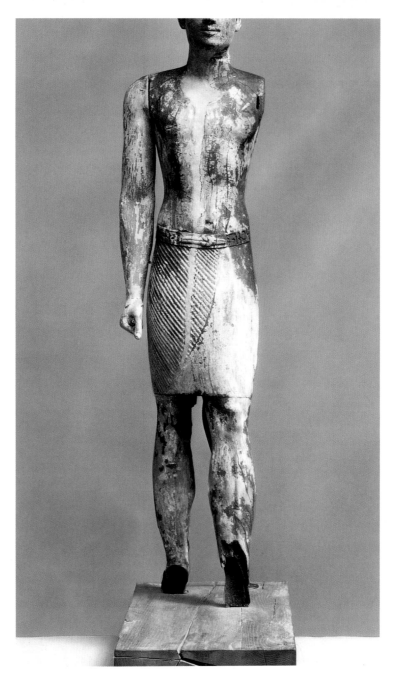

Male underwear through the ages. *Above,* THE ROYAL
ARCHITECT, KA-PU-NESUT (detail), wood, 5th–6th Dynasty,
2750–2475 B.C., Egyptian. The Metropolitan Museum of Art,
Rogers Fund, 1926, New York City. Ka-pu-nesut wears the
schenti, or loincloth. An early example of underwear as outerwear.

Opposite, 1995. Silano, American. Courtesy of the photographer.
More recently, a female model demonstrated a fashion trend
by wearing men's briefs.

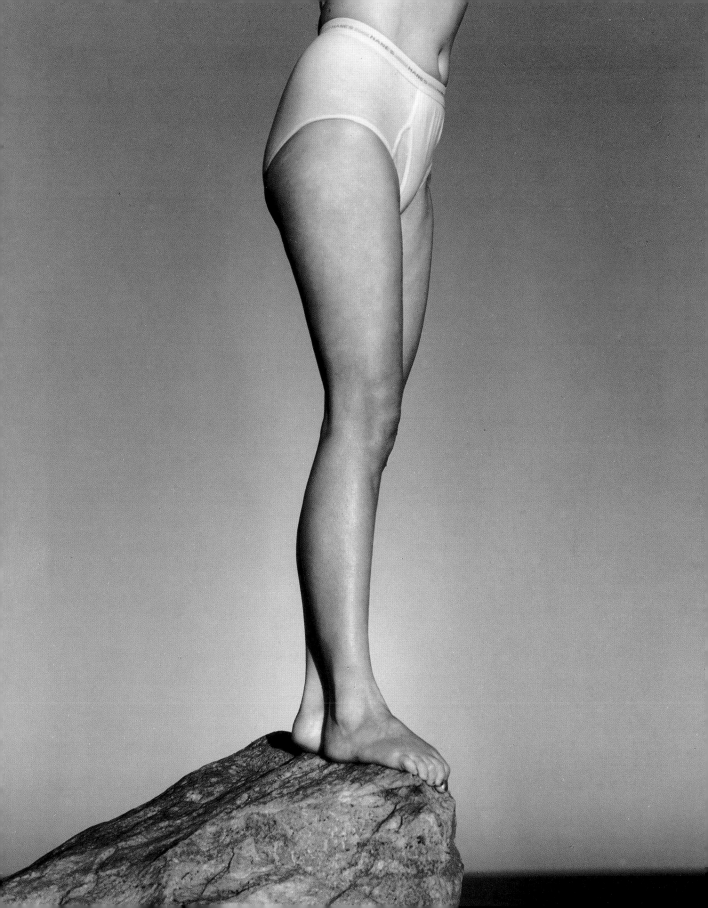

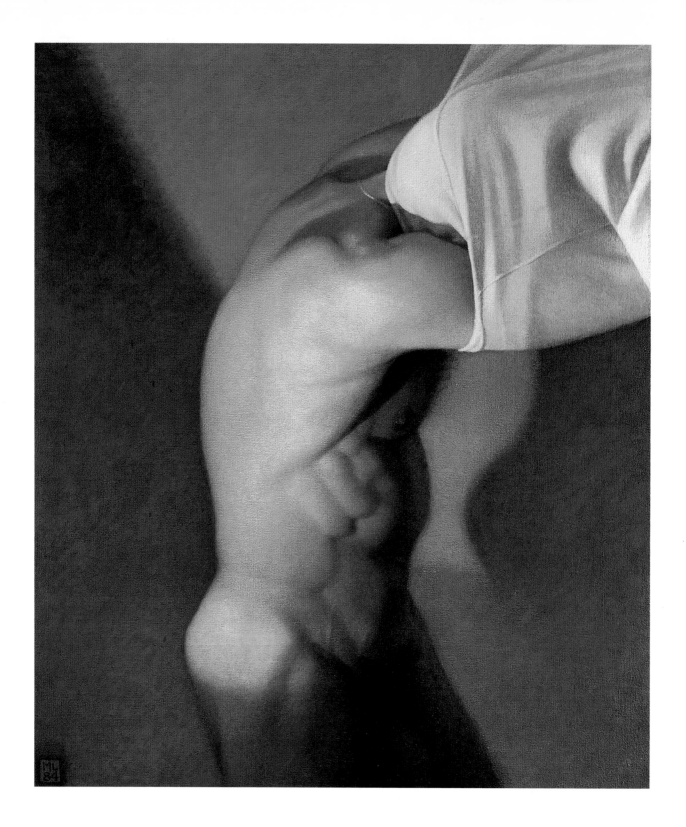

Putting it on, then and now. *Above,* THE BIRTH OF
APHRODITE, detail of the Ludovisi throne, *ca.* 470–60 B.C.,
marble relief, Greco-Roman. Terme Museum, Rome. The
goddess's sheer, pleated tunic could be seen as an early
version of the chemise.

Opposite, MALE TORSO, 1984, oil on canvas. Michael
Leonard, English. Courtesy of the artist.

The camera as voyeur. *Above*, Nastassja Kinski in
Maria's Lovers, 1984. Cannon Pictures. Black is the
lingerie color for a woman of many loves.

Opposite, 1957. Return of the compressed waist.
Fernand Fonssagrives, American. Courtesy of the photographer.
The waist cincher is worn by Lisa Fonssagrives, the
photographer's then-wife and a top model.

2

ON A PEDESTAL

Before women, a wall must be erected: the wall of private life.
Her body is dangerous, both in danger and as a source of danger.
Man risks losing his honor because of it, being led astray,
caught in a trap all the more perilous for being so alluring.

George Duby, *A History of Private Life:*
Revelations of the Medieval World

What is Woman? Wife, mother, daughter, bitch, whore, temptress? Idealized on the one hand and denounced on the other, she's had another role, that of man's property. If the owner of this creature wishes to establish that he can afford a wife or daughter who has no obligation to do menial work, he will take pride in seeing her dressed in such a way that his affluence is obvious; clothes that make it hard to move show that the wearer is rich enough not to have to do very much. On a pedestal, the idealized woman could be celebrated, immobilized, and kept helpless.

Corsets have probably done their part in immobilizing women longer than any other article of underwear; the wearing of tight stays has recurred over the ages and was common throughout most of the sixteenth, seventeenth, eighteenth, and nineteenth centuries. Tightly laced corsets affirmed the inactive status of the women who wore them and were also a metaphor for virtue, despite the fact that courtesans were as tightly corseted as any other woman; it was

thought that ungirdled women might be wanton or "loose." The chastity belt carried the idea to an extreme. A charming medieval invention worn by women to prevent sexual intercourse, it was intended by the Crusaders to guarantee their wives' faithfulness. I found one in the collection of the Carnavalet Museum in Paris, and *Harper's Bazaar* offered one to its readers in 1995, "complete with key," as a gift idea. Just joking, of course.

Aesthetically and in the abstract, antique corsets have a certain charm: rows of tiny hand-stitched seams, intricate embroideries, rims of frothy lace. One marvels at the workmanship. No matter how pretty, however, their mission was to compress the waistline to its tiniest dimensions, and to this end they were reinforced with stays. Most of these were of whalebone but they could also be metal, reed, or double-stitched cording. The first elastic inserts to ease the pain appeared around 1885.

At the end of the nineteenth century some corsets had "bumpers" to support the

"Weery sorry, Mam, but leave yer Krinerline outside."
1858, stereograph, English. Robert Dennis Collection,
The Miriam and Ira D. Wallach Division of Art, Prints
and Photographs, The New York Public Library, Astor,
Lenox and Tilden Foundations. The bulky crinoline had
to be hung from the outside of the public conveyance in
order for the wearer to get aboard.

bustle and some had tabs to hold garters, which in bridal corsets might have sterling silver hardware. The nineteenth century was an extraordinary time in the history of underwear, when girls as young as four were laced into corsets on the theory that it was good for their posture, and no self-respecting woman, rich or poor, would venture out in public without her stays in place.

Usually the corset was worn over a chemise or undershirt that reached to the knees; at the end of the century, corset covers were added. By then women had become as upholstered as the love seats in their drawing rooms. It was not unusual for them to be wearing as many as thirteen undergarments weighing as much as ten pounds. No wonder they were tired at the end of a day.

This concealment had its provocative aspect. The protagonist of Isak Dinesen's short story "The Old Chevalier" describes it: "In those days a woman's body was a secret which her clothes did their utmost to keep ... And underneath all this Eve herself breathed and moved, to be indeed a revelation every time she stepped out of her disguise, with her waist still delicately marked by the stays, as with a girdle of rose petals ..."

Women's corsets were among the earliest manufactured items and became big business. Skeleton corset, reducing corset, bathing corset, maternity and nursing corset, French wedding corset, summer corset—these were just a few of the options. The first Sears, Roebuck catalog, issued in 1896, offers more than a dozen varieties, priced from one dollar to three or four; some are described as "health-promoting."

Below the waist, women were not so much placed on a pedestal as confined in a cage. Consider the farthingale, which first appeared in the Spanish court in the 1470s. It consisted of a tier of hoops sewn into a petticoat, giving the skirt a simple, sloping line. A century later this contraption had grown to enormous proportions and was worn in both France and England, by which time it was as if the woman were standing inside a wheel over which the skirt fell nearly to the floor (you get a good idea of the effect from the portraits of Elizabeth I). Less aristocratic women wore a "bum roll," a padded, sausage–shaped roll that circled the waist, was tied in front, and allowed the long skirt to hang free. The Puritans called farthingales the work of the devil and accused women of hiding men under their skirts.

A period of relatively relaxed dressing followed the demise of the farthingale, lasting until the gradual return of hoops in the first quarter of the eighteenth century. Now, however, the skirt was flat in front and back, volume distributed side-to-side, in extreme cases to as much as fifteen feet. This made it difficult for more than one woman at a time to get through a door or to share a couch. The supporting structures could be made of whalebone or wicker and were called "panniers," after the French word for baskets. Needless to say, it was a costume for the upper classes. Near the end of the century panniers disappeared and fullness was again on the move, now toward the rear of the figure in a kind of bustle.

With the French Revolution all fashion died, along with much of the aristocracy. Then, with the end of the Reign of Terror, for a little more than a decade women enjoyed unprecedented freedom as they adopted a version of classical dress: sheer fabrics, a simpler silhouette with the skirt falling from directly under the bust, and very little underwear.

Soon enough, the waistline began once more to move down toward its normal position, skirts became fuller to make the waist appear smaller, and the corset returned. By the 1840s the bottom half of the female figure had become a miniature dome or oversize lamp shade. What began modestly with a stiffened petticoat, by midcentury had grown to such exaggerated proportions and required so many petticoats that the crinoline or hoopskirt was born. Described in an 1856 patent as a "skeletal petticoat made of steel springs fastened to tapes," it must have seemed liberating compared to the weight of myriad stiffened petticoats. The crinoline's great width gave a woman an impression of unapproachability, but it was also seductive, with a graceful, swaying motion when she walked, giving tantalizing glimpses of ankles. But it was a cumbersome device and an irresistible target for cartoonists and humorists. When the wearer was seated, it rose in front, and when she leaned forward, it rose in back, and in a high

wind it invited indecent exposure. Neither ridicule nor impracticality diminished the crinoline's popularity, however; one English firm made four thousand daily, another produced nine million in twelve years. It took a shift in fashion to do it in.

From the sixteenth through the early nineteenth centuries, women were naked under their chemises. Finally, in the mid-1830s, women for the first time began wearing pantaloons or "drawers," so called because one drew on first one leg, then the other. Though any form of bifurcated women's apparel was frowned on as being masculine, drawers began to be advocated for reasons of health as well as propriety. One English doctor in 1852 recommended them for protection from "our piercing easterly winds." He also said "...they need not descend much below the knees. Thus... being worn without the knowledge of the general observer, they will be robbed of the prejudice usually attached to an appendage deemed masculine."

After 1865, the shapes of hoops altered as skirt fullness again began to migrate to the back of the figure, until by the end of the decade the front was flat and the crinoline had disappeared entirely, to be replaced by the bustle. This invention, which was accompanied by extreme tight lacing, went through various remarkable permutations before it disappeared for good in the 1880s, leaving only corsets and petticoats behind.

The strictness of Victorian times was succeeded by the hedonistic Edwardian era. Voluptuous, mature women were in fashion. The preferred female shape was top heavy, with corsets that threw the bust forward, the hips back, producing the S-shaped curve typical of the period. Paul Poiret claimed to have liberated women from the corset, but took one last fling at confining them when he introduced the hobble skirt. This was so narrow at the ankles that it restricted the wearer to tiny, mincing steps and was sometimes worn with a hobble garter that prevented a full stride that might split the skirt.

World War I brought revolutionary changes as women left the home to do war work, never again to accept the same restricted mobility. Up went the hemlines, and women were free to move, dance, participate in sports, even join the work force, if they so desired. Though free from hampering skirts, they didn't immediately discard all things resembling corsets; even in the roaring twenties they wore "flatteners" to abolish the no-longer-desirable bust. Tight lacing had disappeared and elastic had arrived to soften the pinch, but there were still all-in-ones and girdles that offered varying degrees of control. These were joined after World War II by panty girdles, corselettes, and waist cinchers. Then came miniskirts, made possible by the invention of panty hose, which were eventually to become available with control tops to, yes, smooth the bulges.

So women ultimately climbed down from their pedestals. They exchanged their cumbersome multilayered costumes for streamlined clothing that offers relative freedom and mobility, and they went to work in large numbers. They learned to smoke and drink and, perhaps, tell dirty jokes. But though women have made obvious gains, they've continued to be idealized, romanticized, and to some extent infantilized in popular literature and song. How many would still go along with Irving Berlin's sentiments?

The girl that I marry will have to be
As soft and pink as a nursery,
The girl I call my own
Will wear satin and laces
and smell of cologne.

That was 1946. Now women may jog in sports bra and bicycle shorts but they still keep satin and lace and cologne in their vocabularies, even those most dedicated to a career or with no desire for, or intention of, marriage. Is it possible that a clue to a woman's view of her femininity might be found in her choice of underwear? ■

THE UNEQUAL LOVERS, sixteenth-century German
caricature, hand-colored woodcut. It looks like a chastity belt with
a lock and key, but there's an exchange of gold involved.

Artful exposé. *Right,* L'AIR (the hunting party of the duchess of Lorraine), detail, early seventeenth century, oil on canvas. Claude Deruet (1588–1660), French. Musée des Beaux-Arts, Orléans. Under the complex costumes they wore, even for sport, women of the court had on little or nothing.

Opposite, THE SWING, 1767, oil on canvas. Jean Honoré Fragonard (1732–1806), French. Wallace Collection, London. A voyeur discovers what, if anything, the woman on the swing wears under multiple petticoats.

Among the artifacts, a crinoline from
the Musée de la Mode et du Costume,
Paris, 1985. David Seidner, American.
Courtesy of the photographer.
The once-indispensable
understructure, now as much
a relic as any architectural
fragment, sits for its portrait
in the basement of the Louvre.

Paris in the belle époque. *Above,* 1883, Robert Damachy,
French. Courtesy Janet Lehr, Inc., New York City.
In a pornographic photograph the model reveals what was
under all those petticoats. Nothing!

Opposite, NANA, 1877, oil on canvas. Édouard Manet (1832–1883),
French. Kunsthalle, Hamburg, Germany. A courtesan observed
at her toilette in a painting inspired by Zola's novel.

Coming full circle. *Above,* WINDY DAY, 1860, lithograph, French.
The crinoline was hard to maneuver and in a high wind could be a
threat to public decency, so that drawers or pantaloons became
necessary lingerie in the mid-nineteenth century.

Opposite, Schiaparelli petticoat, 1950, designed by Helen Hunt Bencker
Hoie. Photograph courtesy of the designer. A sheer circular half slip
banded with lace, meant to be worn under big skirts. This was the
beginning of profitable licensing programs through which the stellar
names of French couture were applied to a variety of merchandise
created in America by American designers.

In control—the long-line bra. *This page,* Italian *Vogue,* 1988. David Seidner, American. Courtesy of the photographer. The bra as corselette, shown with sheer, sheer stockings.

Opposite, Veruschka, 1965. Bert Stern, American. Courtesy of the photographer and *Vogue* magazine. One of the first supermodels, wearing lingerie designed specifically for evening—a merry widow corselette and a long, lace-edged half slip.

3

REDESIGNING THE BODY

You may tell her as a friend to reduce her stuffing,
as rumps are quite out in France and are decreasing here,
but cannot quite be given up until the weather grows warmer.
Betsey Sheridan, England, 1786

It appears to be basic human instinct to combine love of one's body and the feeling that it's imperfect and should be changed. "People both dislike their bodies and conceive of them as alluring. As a result, clothing is continually changed or repackaged in an effort to keep the body interesting and attractive." (See Bernard Rudofsky, *The Unfashionable Human Body*, 1971.)

Primitive tribes, too, have their own take on repackaging and alteration, working directly on the body with scarification, tattoos, body painting, and staining. According to Angela Fisher, who photographed them in the 1980s, the Turkana tribe of northern Kenya highlight their bodies with scarring and their faces with paint. "Different styles of body are associated with different tribes. Body art also serves as a detailed sign language, conveying information about the person's age, achievements and social standing ..."

As for tattoos, that fifty-three-hundred-year-old man whose frozen body was discovered near Innsbruck, Austria, had groups of lines tattooed on his lower back and on his ankles, and a cross behind his right knee. And, more recently, according to *New York Times* cultural editor Michael

Kimmelman, King George V, Kaiser Wilhelm II, and Czar Nicholas II all were tattooed. Today's rebels take note. Still, though the bodies of Easter Island women are covered in patterns as creative as those of any fabric designer of our time, and the Japanese have long considered tattoos sexually arousing, in Western civilization tattooing is hardly mainstream.

Far from exposing their bodies, the Victorians practiced concealment, a more subtle form of sexual titillation. Women of the middle or upper classes wore layer upon layer of undergarments, and a bride wrote that she was making her husband "nice, long nightshirts, so that I shan't be able to see any of him." Sexuality, called "animality," was pushed below the surface of polite society; underwear symbolized forbidden fruit. Prudery and prurience were closely related.

Tight lacing, used extensively by the Victorians but not invented by them, was essential to body molding from the Middle Ages onward. It reached its most extreme form in the eighteenth century, its excesses decried by medical men and philosophers alike. In England, John Locke (1632–1704) protested "encasing young bodies in tight corsets reinforced with metal and whale-

TATTOO. Still from the movie *Tattoo*, 1980. Twentieth Century–Fox. Bruce Dern plies his trade as an artist devoted to the ancient art form. Altering the body with paint, tattoos, or scarification has a long history and still exists as a popular fad. Body alteration through undergarments is more common and usually less painful.

bone..." From France, Jean-Jacques Rousseau in *Émile* (1762), predicted the decline of the English race (apparently the English were tight lacing's most ardent advocates) brought about by the practice and lamented that "It is not agreeable to see a woman cut in two like a wasp."

Despite all criticism, the fashion for tiny waists persisted and by the late eighteenth century, the feminine ideal was exaggerated slimness, a pale complexion, and slow, languid movements. Robustness was the antithesis of beauty; a straight back was considered as important as a good dowry in catching an eligible husband, and it was not unusual for young girls to be subjected to what today would be considered child abuse. "Although perfectly straight and well made, I was enclosed in stiff stays with a steel busk in front, while above my frock, bands drew my shoulders back until the shoulderblades met. Then a steel rod with a semicircle which went under the chin, was clasped to the steel busk in my stays." (See Lawrence Stone, *The Family: Sex and Marriage, 1500–1800,* Harper & Row, 1977.) These were the concerns of the upper classes; poor women, for their part, were presumably too occupied with the daily struggle to have time or energy for such fashion niceties. As for underwear, they wore little or none.

Freed from corsets during the Directoire and Empire periods, women resumed tight lacing around 1822, when a small waist again became a prerequisite of beauty. The practice continued throughout the Victorian and Edwardian eras. Then, as noted, with the coming of the First World War women left home to work and drive ambulances, and the pursuit of fashion was out of style.

The arrival of peace brought time once more for frivolity and a need for it; the figure was in for another repackaging as the flapper made her appearance. Waistlines wandered downward, hemlines upward, and the ideal body's newly androgynous shape posed serious problems for those women with the curves so much admired in the Edwardian period. The sinuous little shifts that were all the rage required a boyish figure, and breasts were flattened to achieve it.

From the farthingale to the hoopskirt to the bustle, from the corset to the waist cincher to today's stretch fabrics, what goes on the outside has been shaped by what's underneath, and the female body has been augmented or diminished, laced, pushed, pulled, raised, lowered, and generally altered by underclothes consistent with the fashion of the moment. East or West, clothes have ignored the body's actual conformation, representing a sort of hollow casing for their wearers. The pressure of the undersash and obi worn with the kimono left a discoloration on a Japanese woman's abdomen comparable to the red marks left on a Western woman's midsection by a corset or girdle. Whether as columnar as a kimono or as curvaceous as Dior's New Look, clothes that redesign the body do not take comfort as their first priority.

Our own time has seen enormous changes in the way women dress. Increased mobility, economic necessity, and technological advances in textiles have all contributed to the liberation of the female body. True, from time to time fashion designers try to turn back the clock by trotting out bustiers, corsets, and garter belts (consider the recent reign of the Wonderbra), but most of us are too busy to bother. We choose to wear underwear for reasons of modesty, warmth, cleanliness, comfort, and, oh yes, sexiness. Still, we're never satisfied and continue to redesign our bodies. Our ambivalence toward what we were born with seems to reflect our eternal concern that we are, after all, imperfect. ■

Window dressing. *Above,* BARE ESSENTIALS, 1950. Weegee
(Arthur Felig, 1899–1968), American. Courtesy Janet Lehr, Inc.,
New York City. The strapless bra, in basic black.

Unlaced. *Above, ca.* 1951, the merry widow.
Lillian Bassman, American, for *Harper's
Bazaar.* Courtesy Howard Greenberg Gallery,
New York City.

Opposite, FEMME A SA TOILETTE,
1896, oil on board. Henri de Toulouse-
Lautrec (1864–1901), French. Musée des
Augustins, Toulouse, France. Toulouse-
Lautrec's dual perspective—the viewer of
the picture and the observer within the
picture—introduced a note of fetishism and
voyeurism into getting dressed, or
undressed.

Tight lacing. *Above,* A LITTLE TIGHTER, 1791, engraving.
Thomas Rowlandson (1756–1826), English. The artist satirized
the vanities of eighteenth- and ninteenth-century fashion,
which insured that a "strait-laced" woman would
be hard put to dress herself.

Opposite, Vivien Leigh and Hattie McDaniel in *Gone with the
Wind,* 1939. A David O. Selznick production, Metro-Goldwyn-
Mayer. The fabled 18-inch waist was not easily achieved,
even by a slim Scarlett O'Hara.

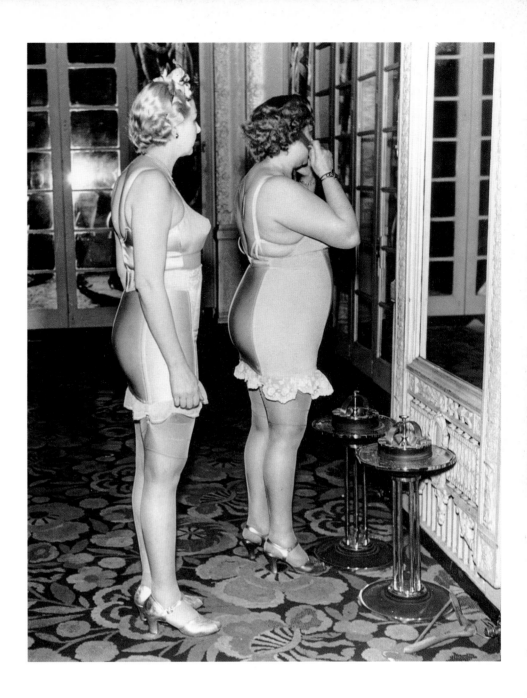

Firm Foundations. *Above,* 1937. Alfred
Eisenstaedt (1898–1995), German. Courtesy *Life*
magazine. © Time, Inc. Corset show at S. Klein's
department store.

Opposite, THE BOWERY SAVINGS BANK, 1945.
Weegee (Arthur Felig, 1899–1968), American.
Courtesy Janet Lehr, Inc., New York City.
Stockings could serve more than one purpose.

4

MY CUP RUNNETH OVER

Uncorseted, her friendly bust
Gives promise of pneumatic bliss.
T. S. Eliot, "Whispers of Immortality"

Push-up bra, no-bra bra, strapless bra —the brassiere as we know it is largely a phenomenon of the twentieth century, though its antecedents can be traced back to ancient Greece and Rome. Who invented the modern bra? There are several claimants of the honor. A "bust improver" of wire and silk appeared in 1886; it looked something like two tea strainers hooked together. Hermione Cadolle, a French corsetiere-seamstress, is said to have designed a version as early as 1889, and Paul Poiret began to build such underpinnings into his clothes a bit later. In 1914 American debutante Mary Phelps Jacobs (helped, it is said, by her French maid) designed and patented a concoction made of two handkerchiefs and some pink ribbons. She eventually turned over the rights to the Warner Corset Company for $1500. Another U.S. patent was granted to Willliam Rosenthal for the first "uplift" brassiere in 1927. His wife, Ida, and her partner, Enid Bàssett, were custom dressmakers, owners of Enid Frocks in Manhattan. Believing that their customers' dresses would fit better over a natural rather than the flattened bust then prevalent, Enid and Ida created the original Maidenform Brassiere. Soon their clients were request-ing extra brassieres, and the Maidenform Company was born. Their campaign, "I dreamed I (you name it) in my Maidenform Bra," became an advertising legend and lasted for more than twenty years.

Even in ancient times some cultures sought to diminish the breasts while others emphasized them. In Minoan Crete women wore laced corsets that supported the breasts but left them bare, while there were Greeks and Romans who banded their breasts with leather strips to flatten them. And by the fifteenth century, at which time women's clothes bore very little relation to the body beneath, a stiff linen underbodice appeared; called a "cotte" or a "body," it was reputedly of Spanish origin. In the sixteenth century this garment began to be made more rigid with slats of whalebone or wood, and England's Elizabeth I went even further, wearing a breast-containing metal corset called an "iron maiden." So the fashion continued with fluctuations between a lesser and a more extreme degree, right up to the French Revolution: tight lacing with the breasts pushed up to swell over at the décolletage.

In France immediately following the end of the Reign of Terror, thin muslin dresses of classical inspiration were given linen lin-

Untitled, *ca.* 1985. David Salle, American, painter-photographer. ©1996/licensed by VAGA, New York City. Courtesy Robert Miller Gallery, New York City. An unexpected pose makes the push-up bra unnecessary.

ings with side tapes that crossed under the breasts, lifting them somewhat. But freedom comes and goes, and soon the Victorian corset arrived; this contained the breasts without delineation, rounding them into a sort of monobosom. Then followed the frillier, lacier camisole of the Edwardian era, referred to in England as a bust-bodice, or "B.B.," boned but unshaped and giving the "pouter pigeon" look one sees in Gibson girl illustrations.

After World War I, cumbersome clothing was declared démodé, the fashion silhouette became softer and more columnar. The ideal flapper of the early 1920s had a slender, boyish figure that reflected the freedom of this new woman. She had been granted the right to vote. She had probably bobbed her hair. However, if she was unlucky enough to have large breasts she contained them as best she could by strapping them down with flannel strips, or by wearing a side-laced bust-flattener or a tight bandeau with no seaming. Slim young things went braless.

By the 1930s it was all right to have two naturally separated breasts. Bras were becoming big business, with firms competing to make lacy confections that were sexy to look at and reasonably durable. And in 1935, thanks to the Warner Company, the era of cup size dawned. Now, from the Alphabet Bra line, a woman could choose the A, B, C, or D cup, whichever conformed best to the size of her breasts. For the underendowed, "falsies" would flesh out any perceived inadequacy.

Government restrictions during World War II put a damper on frivolities such as fancy underwear, but with peace there was the usual reaction: wartime austerity gave way to a new lavishness in many things, and lingerie was no exception. When Christian Dior created his New Look in 1947, feminine curves were back in fashion with a vengeance, emphasizing swelling breasts and small waists, the effect achieved by a battery of padded, push-up bras, corselettes, waist cinchers, and multiple petticoats.

The 1950s brought the pointed bra with exaggerated, cone-shaped cups. Then came the 1960s and a trend toward bralessness. Whether this was in response to the "hippie" movement with its commitment to self-expression, or the new Women's Movement, manufacturers trembled. To wear a bra or go braless became a subject of debate. In 1972, Connecticut-based physician Alfred B. Sundquist entered the fray in a letter to the *Journal of the American Medical Association*: "What do you think of the recent trend among some women of going braless? Should they not be warned by the American Medical Association that a lack of mammary support may lead to the development of pendulous breasts caused by stretching of the fibrous tissue attaching the breasts to the chest?" Doctors rushed to the ramparts, taking one side or the other, but as usual, women ignored the medical men and went their own way.

The "no-bra bra" might be considered a compromise. It arrived in the late 1960s, the inspiration of innovative American designer Rudi Gernreich, and had molded nylon cups with a narrow elastic band that encircled the rib cage. This heralded the soft, body-conscious fluidity of line that has become a hallmark of the latter part of the twentieth century.

Most women still prefer to wear bras,

witness the recent brouhaha over the Wonderbra and the Super-Uplift, push-up bras said to impart the same cleavage that breast implants offer. These have been so successful that the entire industry has benefited, particularly since almost every firm has come up with its own version. In 1994 bra sales doubled over the previous year, and push-ups accounted for 10 percent of the market, far more than they had previously.

Lingerie manufacturers have always given fanciful names to their products, becoming particularly imaginative when it comes to brassieres. "Confidential," "Lovable," "Celebrity," "Young You," "Sensuous Solution," "Jezebel": These are names that suggest short stories.

Bras are now offered in hundreds of styles, colors, fabrics, and sizes. They are acceptably visible under a shirt or jacket; as bustiers they star in public, worn with evening slacks or skirts. Cross-dressers collect them. Preteenagers can't wait to buy them, and the average woman can't wait to take hers off each night. Madonna has turned her Gaultier-designed, cone-shaped bras into signature theatrical costumes. Are brassieres here to stay? Probably—at least as long as they give a lift to women's spirits as well as to their bosoms. ■

"I DREAMED I PAINTED THE TOWN RED IN MY MAIDENFORM BRA." 1962. The Maidenform Museum, New York City. For two decades (1949–69), this campaign converted everyone's worst nightmare—appearing undressed in public—into an effective way to sell bras. It was one of the most successful advertising campaigns ever.

Designer underwear for the liberated body, 1979. John Kloss designed these sheer underthings for Lily of France and also appeared in the advertisement. Susan Shacter, American. Courtesy of the photographer. The combination of lightweight stretch fabrics and contemporary design have brought unprecedented freedom of movement to today's woman.

In the roaring twenties not all women suppressed their curves.
Above, BIBI AT THE HOTEL DES ALPES, CHAMONIX, 1920. Jacques-Henri Lartigue (1895–1986), French. Reproduced by permission of Association des Amis de Jacques-Henri Lartigue, Paris. Surely this pleated underpinning is meant for après-ski and not the slopes.

Opposite, THE GARTER, 1925, pen and ink. John Held, Jr. (1889–1958), American. Courtesy Illustration House, Inc., New York City. In the days before bras and panty hose, the flapper gets dressed.

The recurrent corset. *This page,* 1947,
Christian Dior's New Look corselette.
Lillian Bassman, American, for *Harper's
Bazaar.* Courtesy Howard Greenberg
Gallery, New York City. Dior declared,
"Without foundations there can be no
fashion."

Opposite, BOULEVARD
STRASBOURG CORSETS, 1912.
Eugène Atget (1856–1927), French.
The Museum of Modern Art, New
York City. Corsetry was an important
industry of the nineteenth century. By
the time this photograph was taken,
corset rigidity was softening but wearing
one was still largely de rigueur.

Private lives. *Above,* CITY SUNLIGHT, 1954, oil on canvas.
Edward Hopper (1882–1967), American. Hirshhorn Museum and
Sculpture Garden, Smithsonian Institution, Gift of Joseph H. Hirshhorn Foundation, 1966, Washington. Hopper's ambiguous images
used light, space, and introspective people in intimate situations.

Opposite, 1987. David Seidner, American. *The Village Voice.*
Courtesy of the photographer. As self-absorbed as any Hopper
subject, the waiting woman seems posed between action
and inaction, getting dressed or staying home.

5

GODS AND GODDESSES

Every age remakes the visible world to suit itself.
Geoffrey Squire, *Dress, Art and Society, 1560–1970*

Kings and queens, courtesans and mistresses—there have always been fashion pacesetters, but in early days access to fashion was limited to the privileged upper classes, the few who could afford to emulate the leaders. This select group was joined by a wider audience in the middle of the nineteenth century when women's magazines appeared, but it was not until the twentieth century and the arrival of the movies that most of the civilized world could view a new set of models up close—see how the new stars dressed and, sometimes, undressed. Then, after World War II, television brought these icons into our living rooms and bedrooms.

From portraits and legend we know something about the earliest fashion leaders. In England, Henry VIII and Elizabeth I; in France, Catherine de' Medici and Marie Antoinette—all were style-setters in their day. Queen Elizabeth wore a steel corset. Did she have a bad back? In any case, the members of her court followed suit. Fashion ideas regularly crossed national boundaries, especially when a member of one royal family married into that of another country. In 1533, for example, Catherine de' Medici married France's duc d'Orléans, later Henry II. She brought with her the fashions of her native Urbino, notably its exaggerated petticoats, and her manners

and dress were copied by her court.

As for Marie Antoinette's enormous wardrobe, some has been preserved, including a green satin corset in the collection of the Carnavalet Museum in Paris. Her fashion crossed borders courtesy of her couturière, Rose Bertin, who dressed fashion dolls, complete with multiple undergarments, and carried them around Europe to show to prospective customers.

Actresses once may have been considered somewhat naughty but they've had considerable influence. Tightly laced into corsets that narrowed their midsections and exaggerated their bosoms, Lillian Russell, Sarah Bernhardt, and Lillie Langtry embodied the then-fashionable silhouette; whether they actually led the way or simply epitomized the current ideal, their full-figured curves were much appreciated.

Mae West's hourglass figure, on the other hand, had no connection with the fashion of her time. With her exaggerated walk, smoky voice, and pithy comments, as a sex symbol she was close to a female impersonator, a spoof of the idea that wearing stays made one staid. Heavily corseted, exposing nothing, she exuded sexuality gone comic.

Ideals change and by 1938, when a slim, young Mary Martin went on stage and caused a buzz wearing a lace-trimmed chemise, she was the perfect embodiment of a modern young woman. As may have

Marlene Dietrich. Milton H. Greene (1922–1985),
American, for *Life* magazine, 1952.
©1980 Milton H. Greene Archives.
The legendary legs said it all.

been the case with predecessors, she was not so much leading fashion as reflecting it.

Between the two world wars women designers with strong personalities and a gift for wearing their own clothes had an influence beyond their immediate clientele. The two most prominent were Coco Chanel, with her androgynous figure and personal style, and Elsa Schiaparelli, whose dramatic flare and surrealist borrowings took a more theatrical direction. Schiaparelli's signature perfume bottle was a corseted hourglass shape, an idea recently updated and repackaged for his own fragrance by Jean Paul Gaultier.

In our era the motion picture has been the most profound influence on the way people have thought about clothes. From Theda Bara to Clara Bow, Jean Harlow to Marilyn Monroe to Sharon Stone, there have been stars who became famous for their underwear—and for their lack of it. Lana Turner's sweaters made it clear that her brassiere was doing an outstanding job. The cups were stitched in concentric circles, forming twin cones. In *The Merry Widow* (1952), she wore a strapless black corselette with attached garters, soon widely copied and named for the movie. Howard Hughes claimed that Jane Russell's considerable bosom was held up by a brassiere he designed utilizing his aeronautical engineering skills.

In our cherished Hollywood of the past, underwear often helped tell the story. Alfred Hitchcock used it symbolically in *Psycho* (1960): He first showed Janet Leigh in a white bra and slip after spending time with her lover, then later as a decamping embezzler in black underwear, which she was still wearing in the motel where she was to be killed. Again, Elizabeth Taylor's costume during much of *Cat on a Hot Tin Roof* (1958), is a provocative slip as she

tries to win back her husband's affections. Remember Rita Hayworth in *Gilda* (1946), the personification of glamour as she sits on a bed in that marvelous nightgown? Anyone who ever saw *Gone with the Wind* (1939) can still visualize Vivien Leigh as she was being laced into her corset by Hattie McDaniel, even hear Scarlett O'Hara say of Rhett Butler, "He looks as if he knows what I look like without my shimmy." And while they may not really have been underwear, who can forget Dorothy Lamour in those strapless sarongs?

Male stars, too, affected underwear history. An entire industry took a downturn when Clark Gable took off his shirt in *It Happened One Night* (1934) and turned out to be undershirtless. On the other hand, when Marlon Brando and James Dean flaunted their working class T-shirts in *A Streetcar Named Desire* (1951) and *Rebel Without a Cause* (1955), they exuded sexuality, inspiring more than a generation of imitators. The undershirt was first lost, then reborn, in the movies.

In Hollywood's no-underwear department, there was often more than met the eye. We think of Marlene Dietrich's Las Vegas appearances: Her gown seemed to have been painted on, but the costume was entirely structured, a marvel of body-molding skill. As for Marilyn Monroe in the classic scene in *The Seven-Year Itch* (1955) where her skirt blew up as she stood over a subway grate—she was actually wearing underpants.

Frederick's of Hollywood, an inspired offshoot of Hollywood's glamorous legend, was created by Frederick Mellinger in 1946. He started with a racy catalog and parlayed its success into a chain of more than 175 stores. Now the Frederick's of Hollywood Lingerie Museum in Los Angeles stands as a shrine to underwear, "an anthropological treasure trove of four decades of garments that have shaped the female form." There are bras described as "missiles and snow cones," and a vast assortment of corsets and underpants. The big draw is the lingerie of the stars. There is Cher's black brassiere, Ethel Merman's foundation from *Annie Get Your Gun* (1946); and one of Mae West's white silk and marabou tea gowns recalls her invitation to "Come up and see me some time." Tony Curtis is represented by the padded undergarments that turned him into a woman, a memorable cross-dresser, in *Some Like It Hot* (1959). Madonna's black bustier with gold sequin pasties and black fishnet tights were on display but disappeared during the 1993 Los Angeles riots.

World War II had its own pantheon—not exactly fashion leaders but omnipresent—the pinup girls who turned up on calendars and occupied space over servicemen's bunks and lined the walls of gasoline stations and dry cleaners. Voluptuous young women wearing very little, they were depicted by such illustrators as Vargas and Petty in *Esquire* magazine, as well as by scores of anonymous photographers. Increasingly, lingerie advertisements were published in both fashion and family magazines as well as catalogs. Undergarments were no longer "unmentionable."

There were some thirty years in Hollywood, from the mid-1930s to the mid-1960s, when major movie personalities were recognized throughout the civilized world. They were lionized and imitated; their clothes were copied. By the time the "director's film" appeared, with actors and actresses who looked and dressed more like real people, television had entered the lives of most people in the United States. Things had changed, but not entirely: The TV show *Charlie's Angels* was referred to as "The Jiggle Girls" in honor of its three braless leading actresses, and soap operas such as *Dallas* examined what the rich and famous wore in their boudoirs.

Now, even though reruns of Hollywood classics are shown nightly on television, it's not the same. We used to watch those famous actors and actresses, bigger than life, marveling at their good looks, wondering what they were wearing under those slinky gowns, and how to imitate them without looking silly. Does television with its small screen give the same sense of escape and desire for emulation as the movies? I don't think so. Television's personalities have become as familiar as our own family members (whom we might happen to see in their underwear). Television simply does not have the fashion influence of the big screen.

Our lives have changed, too. The advent of fashion magazines, thick with advertisements, enabled a constantly growing audience to participate in the vagaries of fashion. Lingerie catalogs such as Victoria's Secret are updated versions of Frederick's of Hollywood, and even the staid *New York Times Magazine* features underwear ads. Supermodels are now the stars, young, leggy, slim, selling every new look from waif to Wonderbra. As for the men, male models now take the part of icon, baring their all (or nearly all) for Calvin Klein or Hugo Boss on billboards, buses, and bus shelters.

Both women and men have become more active; they participate in sports; they exercise. Are these sleek, fit creatures the new deities? One thing is certain: these activities have spawned entirely new wardrobes for both sexes, from baggy sweat suits to formfitting bicycle pants and iridescent tights—and with each shift in the outer look there's change in the underpinnings that support it. ■

Updrafts. *Opposite,* Marilyn Monroe caught on a subway grate in *The Seven-Year Itch,* 1955. Twentieth Century–Fox. Few of the many versions of this photograph reveal the fact that the actress was, indeed, wearing underpants.

Below, 1959. A pleated halo for beautiful legs. Fernand Fonssagrives, American. Courtesy of the photographer.

Underwear goes public, according to Hollywood. *Above,* Joan
Crawford and Lester Vail in *Dance, Fools, Dance,* 1931.
Metro-Goldwyn-Mayer. An excellent view of what daring
young things wore under their clothes.

Opposite, Billy Gilbert and Gene Raymond in *Love on a Bet,*
1936. RKO Pictures. The hero is inexplicably out-of-doors
dressed only in boxer shorts and undershirt.

Above, 1938. Mary Martin in the
Cole Porter musical, *Leave It to Me!*
Courtesy of George Meredith. Ingenue
Mary Martin stole the show in a lace-
trimmed teddy.

Rising Stars. *Opposite*, 1994. Molly
Ringwald, actress, in a man's shirt
and briefs. Susan Shacter, American.
Courtesy of the photographer.

The Tease. *Above*, LA TOILETTE BRILLANTE DE
LA DUCHESSE DU GOUT, eighteenth-century
engraving, French. The duchess receives in her boudoir
while being dressed by her maids. In the eighteenth
century there was little time wasted on modesty.

Opposite, 1937. Stripteaser Gypsy Rose Lee. Murray
Korman, American, for *Bachelor* magazine (April 1937).
Museum of the City of New York. Star of Broadway and
Hollywood, this most famous ecdysiast brought
elegance to the art of taking it off.

Underwear at the movies. *This page*,
Elizabeth Taylor and Paul Newman in *Cat
on a Hot Tin Roof*, 1958. Metro-Goldwyn-
Mayer. Her slip was custom-made for her
role in the Tennessee Williams drama.

Opposite, Clark Gable and Norma
Shearer in *Idiot's Delight*, 1939. Metro-
Goldwyn-Mayer. Having shaken the
underwear industry when he showed up
bare chested in *It Happened One Night*,
Gable made amends here by wearing an
undershirt.

The T-shirt goes public. *Above*, 1955, James Dean on the set of *Rebel Without a Cause*. Warner Brothers Pictures.

Opposite, 1951, Marlon Brando as Tennessee Williams's antihero, Stanley Kowalski, in *A Streetcar Named Desire*. Warner Brothers Pictures.

Close quarters. *Above,* Harold Lloyd and William Frawley in
Professor Beware, 1938. Paramount Pictures. Men's underwear
has changed very little since the photograph was taken.

Opposite, "Nylon, a natural traveler." Lillian Bassman,
American, for *Harper's Bazaar,* 1949. Courtesy of the
photographer and Howard Greenberg, Photofind Gallery,
New York City. Dressing on a train in the pointed bra
of the period, and zippered panties.

Sex symbols, 1928, 1990. *This page,*
Mae West in a 1928 Broadway
production of *Diamond Lil.*
Photograph courtesy of Robert
Gable. The corset and the pose spoofed
sex at a time when the feminine ideal
was boyish and slim.

Opposite, Madonna, in concert in
1990, in a Jean Paul Gaultier–designed
corselette with cone-shaped cups.
Courtesy A/P Worldwide Photos. This
became her signature underwear-as-
outerwear costume.

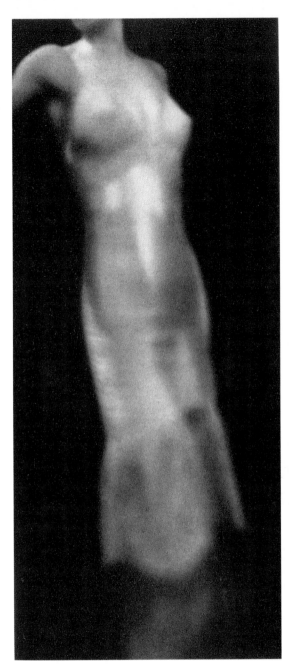

Changing silhouettes, a war and a world apart. *This page,* 1935. From *Harper's Bazaar:* "The line we strive for—a smooth curve over the hips." Solarized photographs, Man Ray (1890–1976), American. Courtesy *Harper's Bazaar.* © 1996 (ARS), New York/ADAGP/Man Ray Trust, Paris.

Opposite, 1951. Short petticoat. Courtesy of the designer, Helen Hunt Bencker Hoie. After World War II, lingerie designers celebrated their liberation from wartime restrictions with a lavish use of color, sheer fabrics, lace.

Legs in perspective. *Opposite,* 1967. Silano, American, for *Harper's Bazaar.* Courtesy of the photographer. Not only were panty hose revolutionary, so was strong color; hosiery was still usually flesh toned.

Below, 1944. Salvador Dalí (1904–1989), Spanish. Surrealist imagery in Bryan Hosiery advertising campaign: "This loveliness will be interpreted in Nylon, when available, fantastically fine, perfectly proportioned."

HOSIERY by BRYAN

At home and at war. *Opposite,* 1942. "Keep the home fires burning." Louise Dahl-Wolfe (1895–1989), American, for *Harper's Bazaar.* Courtesy Staley-Wise Gallery, New York City. Lacy lingerie maintained morale on the home front.

Below, ca. 1943, Tyrone Power hangs them out to dry in an official Marine Corps photograph. When the Twentieth Century–Fox star entered the service during World War II, he had to wash his own skivvies just as everyone else did.

OFFICIAL MARINE CORPS BASE PHOTO

6

SPORT, DANCE, HEALTH, FITNESS

Our mother, she is a sportswoman, an athlete,
a ballroom divinity. She is alternately a horsewoman,
a huntress, a bold and skillful swimmer.
Alan Bell, 1873

Alan Bell's mother might not be considered an unusual woman today, but in 1873, when seven to ten pounds of underwear was considered a normal complement, she was clearly worth shouting about. Few women moved about as freely as she, and it would be nice to know what she wore under all her various outfits, but we can only consider the acceptable outerwear and known underwear of the period and make a guess.

Whatever she wore, it would have been far different from what is worn by her modern counterpart or from what was worn in classical antiquity, when sport, dance, health, and fitness were glorified, clothing was simple and unbinding, and both men and women had freedom of movement and exercised in the gymnasium, wearing very little if anything at all. It was more common for men than women to participate in sports, but a Sicilian mosaic from the fourth century A.D. shows a woman in what looks like a modern two-piece bathing suit, carrying what resemble jogger's weights. As women's clothing became more structured, their movements were increasingly restricted and their demeanor became more formal; it finally became virtually impossible to participate in activities that required more than minimal movement.

Dance, defined by the *Oxford English Dictionary* as "To skip, hop, or glide with measured steps and rhythmical movements of the body, usually to the accompaniment of music, either by oneself or with a partner or in a set," also reflects the costumes and customs of time and place. This is especially true of social dancing, which in periods when female costume was rigid and immobilizing, was stylized and stiff. The minuet is perfectly appropriate for a corseted woman wearing a big skirt—grasping his partner's hand, a man could put her through the stately paces of a dignified dance without touching her body. The waltz was considered daring because the man held his partner's waist, however tightly corseted—and there was always the exciting possibility of an ankle revealed as petticoats swirled. Folk dances in all cultures have traditionally been more active, revealing layers of underwear and flashes of legs.

In France the bawdy cancan dancers, originally laundresses and other working women, kicked high to reveal their stockings, garters, petticoats, drawers, and sometimes more. The tantalizing glimpses of bare flesh at the tops of their hose were pretty racy in a culture where women's

Marisa Berenson. Bert Stern, American, for *Vogue* magazine, 1965. Courtesy of the photographer. The model-cum-actress wears a one-piece exercise suit by Rudi Gernreich inspired by a dancer's leotard and tights.

skirts reached to the floor and their undergarments were multiple. The dance was eventually transferred to the music-hall stage. Artists such as Toulouse-Lautrec depicted the hectic atmosphere of the music hall and showed both dancers and prostitutes in deshabille. Degas also used whores as subject matter, showing them in the brothel in a state of undress. But even his ballet dancers appear to be corseted above their tutus, so it's little wonder that such pioneering dancers of the early twentieth century as Loie Fuller and Isadora Duncan caused a sensation. Ungirdled and free-spirited, they went daringly barefoot and swirled their many-scarved costumes around their unfettered bodies. The biblical Salome of the seven veils may well have been their aesthetic ancestor.

Through the centuries women who would be athletes have had to struggle for the right to exercise in public. A few rode horseback for sport as well as travel and then, and only then, was some form of pants acceptable, usually worn as underwear, since pants were considered uniquely masculine garments until the mid-nineteenth century. Toward the end of the century, bicycling and skating were introduced as sports in which women could participate and there was some accommodation of dress, including the elimination of corsets and the wearing of bloomers.

Bloomers, billowing trousers derived from a Turkish woman's costume and named for their nineteenth-century advocate, Amelia Bloomer, were an early attempt at sensible dressing, at first derided by cartoonists and resisted by all but a handful of dress reformers. Eventually, the realization that something of the sort was necessary if women were to participate in sports led to their adoption by bicyclists.

Bloomers evolved into the hated gym suit and finally, shortened, went undercover and were reclassified as underwear. When women took to sport, the demise of underwear and multiple petticoats was inevitable; then as females gathered in their skirts to climb aboard the newly invented automobile, the death knell of such voluminous gear was finally sounded.

Active sportswear did not happen overnight. Croquet could be played by tightly laced women, but action sports cried out for something new. As petticoats and corsets were discarded, hems were shortened, divided skirts became acceptable, and new elasticized fabrics were introduced. Early tennis outfits were adaptations of daily wear; they may have been daring at the time but look ludicrous today. How could women play in them? At Wimbledon, each change caused a mild scandal, from Suzanne Lenglen's white stockings and mildly shortened skirts of the 1920s to "Gorgeous Gussie" Moran's one-piece tennis dress in 1959, with its flirtatious lace-trimmed underpants. Gussie's panties made headlines worldwide.

As for bathing suits, Mack Sennett's early bathing beauties wore stockings, bloomers, long jersey tunics, shoes, and a kind of mop cap. A look at the Miss America beauty contest, starting in 1927, shows the slow but constant change in bathing suits, as well as of idealized body types. Legs have grown longer as more thigh is exposed; bosoms seem higher and rounder; exercise and changed nutritional habits have resulted in taller, leaner, fitter young women.

Women's involvement in active sports has altered their underwear as well as their bodies and their lives. And as the sports mode controls sunlight choices, the dance mode affects the lamplight one. Some women still indulge in ball gowns with expansive skirts more suitable for the minuet than any dance more recent, but the constricted space of a nightspot demands minimalist, body-conforming clothes that move with the dancer and require a minimum of lingerie. Dance crazes, from the shimmy to the jitterbug to the twist, from the hustle to hip-hop, have fostered their own appropriate underthings, more for jitterbugging and hip-hopping, fewer and sleeker for less athletic performances. For more formal ballroom dancers, from Irene Castle to Ginger Rogers, high style and elegance were the message, and there was undoubtedly beautiful, supple lingerie under those floating gowns.

It's been only a hundred years since a fashion revolution started to liberate women's bodies from the bizarre costume conventions that had virtually immobilized them for centuries. During this period women have gained the vote, become economic partners with their husbands, learned to swim, jog, play tennis and golf, scuba dive, and hang glide. Women now participate in marathons and road races; they do aerobics and pump iron. And they have adopted lingerie that suits their ever-widening range of interests, their ever more active lives. ■

AU SALON, 1879, monotype.
Edgar Degas (1834–1917), French. Musée Picasso, Paris.
Nude or, more provocatively, half undressed in corset or
camisole and stockings, prostitutes await clients.

The knees have it. *Opposite*, COUSIN SIMONE, 1910. Jacques-Henri Lartigue (1895–1986), French. Courtesy Association des Amis de Jacques-Henri Lartigue, Paris. Cycling in its various forms made a strong case for wearing bloomers.

Below, Clara Bow in *It*, 1927. Paramount Pictures. The "It girl" in a carnival scene that may have been the inspiration for the Jazz Age slang expression "the bee's knees."

Underlining the sporting life in
Life. Above, 1950. Wrestlers at the
gathering of the Braemar Royal
Highland Society. The definitive
answer to the question of what
Scotsmen wear under their kilts.

Opposite, 1955. Italian tennis player
Lea Pericoli lost her first match at
Wimbledon, but the crowd loved her
while she lasted. Both photographs
courtesy The Bettmann Archive.

Coming-out parties. *Opposite,* ST. MORITZ, 1913. Jacques-Henri Lartigue (1895–1986), French. Courtesy Association des Amis de Jacques-Henri Lartigue, Paris. The predicament of this hapless skier reveals the very modern-looking briefs that underpinned her ski pants.

Below, 1959. Hosiery advertisement. Fernand Fonssagrives, American. Courtesy of the photographer. Petticoat and stocking-clad legs vie for attention.

7

FAST FORWARD

I'll put a girdle round about the earth in forty minutes.
Shakespeare, *A Midsummer Night's Dream,* 2.1

Today's woman can dress in a matter of seconds. She hooks her bra (elasticized and easily washed), draws on her panty hose (with or without "tummy control"), dons a T-shirt or sweater, skirt or jeans, shoes or boots, and is ready to go. She has plenty of other underwear options: an androgynous cotton undershirt and knitted cotton briefs; a push-up bra that lifts her breasts and emphasizes her cleavage; a silken teddy that recalls custom-made French underwear of the 1920s; a garter belt from Victoria's Secret that tops a lace thong; and of an evening, a boned, quilted bustier that is meant to be seen.

Technology has changed our lives immeasurably. That same speedy dresser has probably had a quick shower, used a flush toilet, brushed her teeth, blow-dried her hair, and applied her makeup, all in a matter of minutes. A century ago a woman's preparations for the day could have taken up the entire morning and required the assistance of a lady's maid. But the changes are not quite as innovative as we think.

Spinning fiber into yarn and weaving yarn into cloth are technical skills that go back five thousand years or more: to the banks of the Nile for linen and cotton, to China for silk. And the use of dyes to color fabrics dates at least to ancient Persia. As for hygiene, there was running water in the palace at Knossos; the Romans built aqueducts and installed communal baths across their empire; there were underground waste removal troughs in Pompeii.

But during the Dark Ages that followed the collapse of classical civilization, these civilized refinements and attention to personal hygiene languished in western Europe and were slow to return. As late as the eighteenth century in the French court, then considered the grandest in Europe, bodily cleanliness left much to be desired. In houses without running water, lit only by candles and heated by open fires, bathing was an event not undertaken lightly. Chemises were rarely removed, serving as basic day and night wear for both sexes. Clothes were aired rather than washed or dry-cleaned. Perfume was used as much to mask body odors as it was as an aphrodisiac. As early as the sixteenth century women wore a scented pomander between the breasts—a reminder of which custom can be found today in an embroidered rosette at the center of some brassieres—and perfume-infused wax cones were inserted into elaborate coiffures. Contemporary accounts

"Become a Buff Buff," 1974. Neal Barr, American, for a Vanity Fair advertising campaign. Courtesy of the photographer. The invention of spandex made possible lightweight body shapers such as this.

describe the lice that plagued wearers of multilayered undergarments and intricate hairstyles that were not disturbed for weeks; devices such as back scratchers were used to reach into infested hairdos and under corsets to relieve the itching. Wig-wearing men commonly shaved their heads.

In 1820, Francis Place (1771–1854), the English radical reformer, described the ignorance, immorality, drunkenness, and depravity of the late eighteenth century, not to mention the lack of personal hygiene. "Women wore stays made of bone and leather which lasted for decades, day and night, without being washed. They also wore quilted petticoats, never washed, until they disintegrated. The spread of cheap and easily washed underclothing in the early nineteenth century has done wonders in respect to cleanliness and health care." Moreover, he continues, "Any improvement could be attributed to the introduction of cotton underclothing, which revolutionized personal cleanliness." Overstatement? Perhaps, but there's little doubt that the Industrial Revolution fostered a striking elevation of both manners and morals. The history of costume is entwined not only with technical developments in fabric and design but also to some extent with improved standards of cleanliness and the introduction of indoor plumbing and central heating.

The Industrial Revolution, which coincided with the reign of Queen Victoria in England, gave rise to a substantial middle class, and as prosperity increased in the nineteenth century, women of the lower classes could afford to copy the dress of the well-to-do. The crinoline, for example, was worn by female factory workers of the 1860s regardless of its impracticality.

What were some of the inventions that revolutionized the way people dress? Certainly the application of waterpower to yarn-spinning machinery; Eli Whitney's invention of the cotton gin in 1793; the sewing machine, invented in 1845; all these made possible mass production of cotton yarns and fabrics and, eventually, of finished garments.

In an early example of industrial espionage, Samuel Slater left his native England in disguise, arriving in Providence, Rhode Island, in 1789. There, from memory, he reproduced the complicated machinery used in manufacturing cotton yarn, and harnessed waterpower to make the first power-spun yarn in this country. This was the beginning of the textile industry in the United States and of its leadership in mass production.

It was not until after the Civil War that undergarments and blouses began to be mass produced; until then the only articles of underwear that had been manufactured were corsets and crinolines; body linen had continued to be made at home, by hand. Between 1840 and 1875, more than seven thousand patents were issued in the United States for various sewing-related machines and accessories. The invention of the sewing machine, of power looms, of powerful machines that could cut myriad layers of cloth at a time, all these, plus a great influx of immigrants from Ireland and southeastern Europe, eager for employment at any wage, gave impetus to the growth of this new garment industry and provided it with workers. A shirt that had taken twelve or twenty-four hours to make by hand could be machine-sewn in little more than an hour.

Up until the mid-nineteenth century, natural fibers—cotton, linen, wool, silk— were the basis of all textiles, but then the development of synthetics began, and improvements were made in existing natural materials. In 1839, while searching for a method that would keep rubber from melting in hot weather, Charles Goodyear developed vulcanization, the process that allows the latex fiber to stretch and then contract; this was the first step toward elastic fabrics and reasonably comfortable corsets. Then, in the 1850s, came the first synthetic polymers, which would ultimately overwhelm all other fibers used in underwear fabrics. A cellular cotton was developed in England in 1887 and used to make "healthy underwear that could breathe."

The pace of inventions continued to pick up in the twentieth century. Rayon was invented in France by René de Réaumur in 1905, using synthetic resins; he called it "art silk." Viscose rayon, made from wood pulp or cotton waste, has been produced since 1911; and in 1919, Lastex, a core of latex wrapped with another fiber, arrived on the scene. Light in weight, easily washed, it was an instant success and was to revolutionize the underwear business. No longer would a woman have to be hooked and laced into her corset. Instead, she could pull on or zip up her two-way-stretch girdle without assistance. And then came nylon and polyester for even lighter and more washable textiles that were wrinkle-proof as well. Not only were fabrics becoming more user-friendly, the invention of the washer-dryer just after World War II brought new ease and efficiency to the laundry process, making it that much simpler to be clean from the skin out.

This period of explosive technological growth in fibers and fabrics totally changed fashion. As underwear went through sea changes from tightly laced to light, flexible, and easily cared for, women's clothes became more fluid, and certainly more comfortable. Bodies changed as women joined the workforce, and changed even more as they became increasingly conscious of healthful eating and the joys of fitness. The "good old days" are talked about with nostalgia but on closer examination leave a great deal to be desired. And the advances in technology that have brought improved hygiene and easier living are part of a technological revolution still in progress as we reinvent, recycle, and rethink our resources.

Women's underwear, still expensive when custom-made, can be both attractive and affordable when mass-produced. Hundreds of companies compete, ranging from respected firms that go back more than half a century to newcomers with sassy names and innovative ideas who have just climbed aboard. Intimate apparel is a billion-dollar industry. Stern-sounding foundations, all-in-ones, and body smoothers have been replaced by lightweight controllers with euphemistic names—Shape-suit or Secret Hug or "I-Can't-Believe-It's-a-Girdle." There are also undershapers, body-briefers, and a bifurcated something called a pantliner that goes from waistline to midcalf. Waist cinchers are with us even now, and petticoats that flatten the stomach, new Miracle Boost panties that shape the buttocks, bellybands and butt boosters (don't ask what they do). Intimate apparel may still be confining, but its vocabulary has a great deal of give and take.

Underwear is now equal opportunity. An older woman may choose the security of a boned all-in-one corset, with garters to hold up her stockings, or she may choose bra, panties, and opaque panty hose with elasticized tops. (All are available from the Sears catalog.) Yet again she may wear the same underthings as her granddaughter. Then there are those who agree with fashion designer-seer Bonnie Cashin, who in 1959 declared underwear obsolete. What do you think? Keep your underwear as your own deep secret or let it all hang out—the option is yours. ∎

Innovations in underthings, 1967. Neal Barr, American.
Courtesy of the photographer and *Harper's Bazaar.* The
bodysuit and the introduction of panty hose changed
forever the way women dress.

An early version of the all-in-one, 1945. Louise Dahl-
Wolfe (1895–1989), American. Courtesy of *Harper's
Bazaar* and Staley-Wise Gallery, New York City. Then-
model Lauren Bacall photographed in the Fifth Avenue
apartment of Princess Gourielli (Helena Rubenstein).

The antique and the modern. *Opposite,* 1967.
Neal Barr, American, *Harper's Bazaar.* Courtesy of the
photographer. The ideal figure, clad in the era's usual
underpinnings of bra and panty girdle.

Below, 1957. Tana Hoban, American. Courtesy of the
photographer. The adolescent model wears an antique
eyelet-embroidered petticoat.

Where the wild things are. *Above,* Anne Bancroft and Dustin Hoffman in *The Graduate,* 1967. Embassy Films, a Mike Nichols–Lawrence Turman production. Bancroft's jungle-print bra and panties fit her sophisticated older-woman character, while Hoffman, young college graduate, wears regulation boxer shorts.

Opposite, 1963. "Flowers in your dressing room." Bert Stern, American, for Vanity Fair advertisement. Courtesy of the photographer. The soft, shaped bra is less pointed than in the 1950s, and the panty girdle performs its slimming task relatively painlessly.

8

THE MALE ANIMAL

*In species after species, the females are sensible
in their size, attire and accessories,
while the males are often oversize, overdressed
and burdened with awkward appendages
and seemingly foolish patterns of behavior.*

Charles Darwin, *On the Origin of Species,* 1859

In the animal kingdom, the male is usually more ostentatiously colorful than the female, presumably making him more attractive to potential mates. Male humans up until the last two centuries dressed with as much brio as women. But then their clothes, and their underwear in particular, developed along singularly colorless lines. The present and future, however, would seem to offer considerably wider options.

Differences in anatomy have always dictated basic differences between men's and women's undergarments. Women's underwear has been more about form, often to the point of distortion, a pretty covering featuring lace, ruffles, handwork, and sheer fabrics, and emphasizing sexuality rather than practicality. Men's underwear has always been primarily functional, conforming to the body's shape, and made of sturdy, protective fabrics.

The oldest example of men's underwear, the loincloth, dates back to the cave man. It was worn by the fifty-three-hundred-year-old man found frozen in the Alps, and according to an account by Abel Hugo, brother of Victor, was still worn in 1835 by the shepherds of the Landes area in southwest France. King Tut's loincloths were described by experts studying them some

fifty years after their discovery in his tomb as "a long piece of linen shaped like an isosceles triangle with strings coming off the long ends." These were tied around the hips, and the length of cloth hanging down in back was brought forward between the legs and tucked over the tied strings from the outside in. As previously noted, Japanese prisoners taken in World War II were similarly undergarbed. Traditional Chinese male underwear is a cut-and-sewn version of the loincloth, a diaperlike brief tied in front, with two cross-panels.

The Romans were exposed to bifurcated garments at least as early as the second century B.C., when one of their armies was defeated by the Teutons. These men wore a short tunic, under which went breeches or baggy trousers, sure proof to the Romans that they were "barbarians." Contrary to the usual result, instead of the defeated people adopting the conquerors' mode it was here the other way around and the invaders soon began to wear something resembling Roman dress. However, both long and short trousers were gradually accepted by the Romans, adopted first by soldiers, who recognized their practicality. By A.D. 481–752, the Franks, who at that time ruled France, wore breeches, or *braies*; these ended at the

Brief briefs, 1995. Photograph by Herb Ritts, American,
for Hugo Boss European advertising campaign.
Courtesy Hugo Boss. A contemporary version of the
archetypal male underwear.

knee or were long and cross-gartered. Either way, they went under a knee-length tunic. In conservative Rome, meanwhile, both men and women continued to wear similar layers of tunic plus toga, although men sometimes wore an extra undertunic and their tunics were usually shorter than women's to accommodate their more active lives.

It was much later that male and female attire diverged dramatically. Men shortened their tunics and exposed their legs in breeches while women continued to hide their legs under long skirts that reached to the ground. In the eleventh century the nobility wore fitted breeches under tunics that could reach to midcalf or below; for the lower classes breeches were loose and baggy and tunics stopped at the knee. By the twelfth century the nobility's breeches had shrunk still further to become invisible drawers, while the laboring classes made do with breechclouts, i.e., loincloths. The tunic continued to diminish into the fifteenth century, soon becoming a doublet, and as men's legs were newly revealed, mobile and independent, their garb was becoming increasingly colorful and flamboyant. The top of the costume was form-fitting and laced in front. Stiffened "stomachers" with pointed front panels were worn by both men and women. Underneath, both sexes wore chemises that resembled shirts and also served as nightdress. (French costume historian Cecil St. Laurent holds the contrary view that people slept in the nude for centuries, but clearly, nobody knows.) The outer garment was slashed to reveal glimpses of these "undershirts," also visible at the wrists and neck.

With the development of plate armor in the twelfth century, padded linen linings evolved as protection against the harsh metal, and padded loincloths were added for horsemen. These were the real antecedents to what has been worn by men as underwear ever since.

Both males and females wore stockings that could be decorated with embroidery and even jeweled. Early hose stopped at the knee but by the twelfth century had risen to midthigh, where they were pulled over the breeches. Later, men's hose, often tied below the knees with ribbons or tapes, the decorative precursors of garters, were attached to the breeches, which in turn were laced to the doublet. Women's hose were covered by skirts that reached the floor. In the beginning, stockings were cut from cloth, either linen or wool, and shaped to the leg, knitting being little known until the time of Elizabeth I. The introduction of knitted hose meant greatly improved fit.

By the sixteenth century the male codpiece was dramatically apparent. What began as a simple, three-cornered gusset in the upper part of the trunk-hose, short full breeches reaching about halfway down the thigh, was enlarged into a stiff, stuffed protuberance, echoing and emphasizing the shape of the male organ. A costume historian has written, "The entire male population above the age of three appeared to be suffering from a severe case of priapism." These exaggerated codpieces were said to be used as storage areas for coins and sweets, much like a women's purse. Their lineal descendant, the jockstrap, is still worn by male athletes and dancers as protection for their genitals. In the world of ballet, for example, it is stuffed, usually with women's sanitary napkins, not only to protect the dancers' private parts but as a symbol of masculinity.

Men's clothes in the sixteenth century were every bit as embellished as women's, multilayered, and brilliantly colored. While outer clothes could be made of silk, satin, lace, or taffeta, what underwear existed was made of, and referred to, as "linen," probably because it was the only item of clothing that was washed. Chemises were thigh-length and stuffed into the outer layer of clothing. Pantaloons and garters went over stockings, and the sleeves and tops of chemises were exposed. Men were known to wear padding to flesh out their calves, as a "fine leg" in a man was considered most desirable. Henry VIII, with his plumed hat, broad shouldered robe, slashed and decorated doublet, hose, beribboned garters, and aggressive codpiece, is the image of masculine power.

This may be the moment to answer the inevitable question, "What does a Scotsman wear under his kilt?" The early answer was "trews," a Celtic garment consisting of loose-fitting breeches and hose, knitted into one piece and worn by Highlanders as they walked the moors. We can assume that current kilt wearers have more options.

With the French Revolution and the demise of the French court, the English aristocracy became the models for male fashion. As landed gentry, they rode around their property, and what they wore, especially the Englishman's country dress, was casual and comfortable. For all except formal occasions and court appearances, knee breeches gave way to less formfitting trousers that were tucked into boots.

There were dandies, of course, who did not subscribe to this relaxed mode, most notably Beau Brummel, who prided himself on the smooth, wrinkle-free fit of his clothes. He was known particularly for his meticulously kept linen undergarments at a time when cleanliness was not given a high priority.

Throughout the centuries, some men, particularly in the military, have worn some form of corset to facilitate the upright stance consistent with a warrior cult. As recently as 1908 the Sears, Roebuck catalog offered a "male military corset giving the straight front effect that is so much admired." There were two versions, one costing ninety-two cents and the other $1.50. Some mail-order catalogs still offer the male equivalent of the panty-girdle, touting it as "health-giving" but clearly counting on the vanity factor to attract buyers.

By the 1830s underdrawers made of flannel were being worn by men, and by the end of the century some had adopted the three-piece knitted wool sleep suit—helmet, crewneck sweater, and long drawers with feet—advocated by German reformer Dr. Gustav Jaeger. Wool had previously been considered a refuge for vermin, but personal hygiene was improving and Dr. Jaeger was persuasive. The English, in particular, subscribed to his theory that wool rather than linen made the perfect undergarments. John L. Sullivan, who hailed from chilly Boston, wore long wool drawers as a boxing outfit, and in the United States these became known as long johns. These were available as separate vests and ankle-length drawers, or as all-in-one-piece union suits. The 1895 Montgomery Ward catalog offered them for ten cents a suit, in "natural wool color gray, and the very popular red." Union suits, either knee or ankle length, were buttoned down the front and had drop seats. The epitaph on a nineteenth-century tombstone reads: "Beneath this stone, a lump of clay, lies Uncle Peter Daniels / Too early in the month of May, he took off his winter flannels."

Undershorts, both boxer and Jockey, are twentieth-century arrivals, their derivation clear from their names. Topped with ribbed cotton undershirts or T-shirts, they're often worn for sleeping as well as for day, although pajamas still hold their own at night, and the Victorian nightshirt, once virtually obsolete, has had something of a resurgence. Jockey shorts in cotton knit (the name is commonly used generically although it's been trademarked) are the most obvious descendants of the loincloth. Briefs, which have become popular as stretch fabrics made this minimal garment more comfortable, are even briefer. Such mail-order catalogs as He Man offer a broad spectrum of styles and fabrics. For the conservative man concerned more with comfort than sleekness, the Brooks Brothers white cotton boxer shorts with button fronts and back panels have remained the shorts of choice but are increasingly hard to find. Updated versions in Sea Island cotton are available from Ermenegildo Zegna for an extraordinarily high price and more modestly priced models from the Lands' End catalog, "silky, light, luxurious." We are told that Brooks Brothers now offers a panoply of other choices but only a limited selection of its own classic.

No report on contemporary underwear would be complete without mention of Calvin Klein, whose bold and provocative advertising brought the subject out into the open in the 1980s, and sometimes makes it seem omnipresent. While the no-frills Fruit of the Loom firm once dominated the men's underwear business in the United States, designer labels such as Tommy Hilfiger and Ron Chereskin, and of course, Calvin Klein, now offer a range of choice. There's much more to men's underwear these days than sedate white, blue, or muted stripes; designers such as Nicole Miller and Gene Meyer have transferred their lively graphic designs to men's furnishings, including underpants. And then there's "Joe Boxer," real name Nicholas Graham, who has brought wit and designer graphics to the milieu: hearts, buffalo plaid (with Velcro-affixed raccoon tail), etc. In 1985 the United States Secret Service confiscated a thousand pairs of his shorts on grounds that they violated forgery laws; they were silk-screened with $100 bills. According to Mr. Graham, "Underwear is . . . still one of those issues people snicker about. There's this whole connotation that it's a secret subject, and that's part of its appeal. You can make it funny."

Unlike women's underwear with its sexy aspect, the primary purpose of men's underthings is still cleanliness and comfort, with the cliché that preppies choose boxer shorts, working class men wear Jockey shorts, and briefs are preferred by gays. But those lines clearly no longer hold. As in the field of women's underwear, anything goes and the male animal may well be regaining his traditional flamboyant place in the animal kingdom—at least in what he chooses to wear under his suit. ■

Dressing or undressing outdoors? 1890. English. Robert Dennis
Collection, Miriam and Ira D. Wallach Division of Art, Prints
and Photographs, The New York Public Library, Astor,
Lenox and Tilden Foundations. The complicated ritual of
dressing out of doors provided greater erotic stimulation
for the stereograph viewer.

The timeless briefs. *This page*, ST. SEBASTIAN, from a polyptych of the Misericordia, fifteenth century, tempera on wood. Piero della Francesca (*ca.* 1420–92), Italian. Pinacoteca Comunale, Sansepolcro, Italy. The martyr's briefs seem completely modern, their design little changed in the nearly six centuries since this picture was painted.

Opposite, ISCHIA, Italy, 1955. Herbert List (1903–1975), German. © Herbert List Estate. Courtesy Robert Miller Gallery, New York City. Mid-twentieth century, a tank top has joined the briefs.

Underwear as swimwear. *Above,* fifteenth century. From an
illuminated manuscript, *History of the Great Alexander.* Musée
du Petit Palais, Paris. The bathers' undershorts are
close kin to today's boxer shorts.

Opposite, AMMERSEE, Germany, 1950. Herbert List
(1903–1975), German. Copyright © Herbert List Estate.
Courtesy Robert Miller Gallery, New York City.
For impromptu swimming, little has changed.

Greetings! You're in the army now. *Above*, Arlo Guthrie (in hat)
in *Alice's Restaurant*, 1969. United Artists. Briefs appear to be
the underwear of choice for the folk singer–protester of the
Vietnam War and his fellow recruits.

Opposite, Elvis Presley weighing in, 1958. Don Cravens,
American. Courtesy *Life* magazine. © Time, Inc. Elvis, too,
prefers briefs, while a fellow recruit goes for boxer shorts.

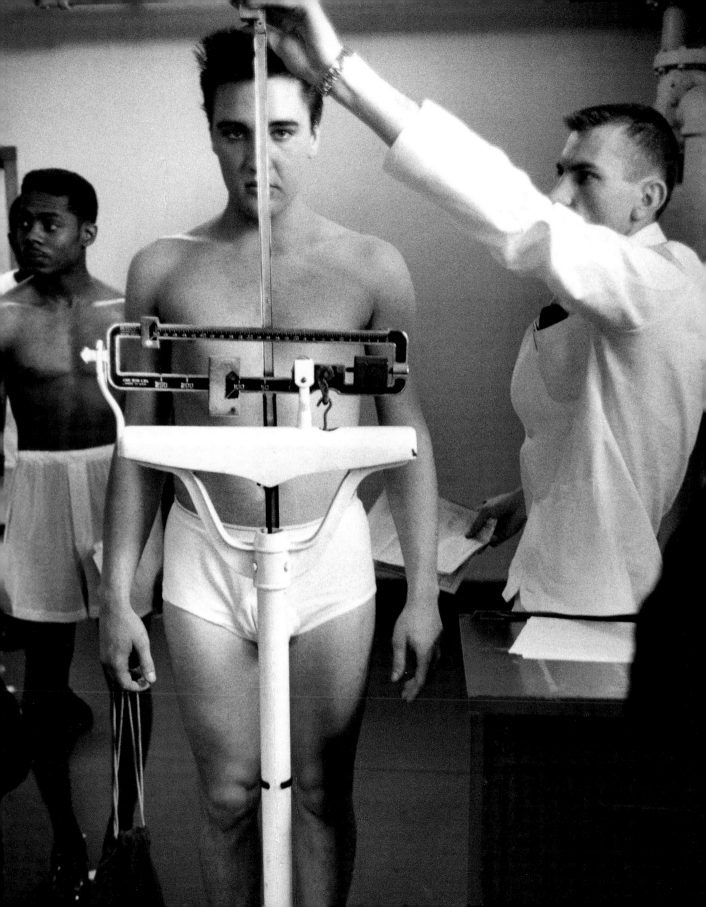

Getting dressed. *This page,* EIGHT O'CLOCK (MORNING) #2, 1917,
watercolor on paper. Charles Demuth (1883–1935), American.
Wadsworth Atheneum, Hartford. The collection of Philip L. Goodwin
through James L. Goodwin and Henry Sage Goodwin.

Opposite, Dick Powell and Ruby Keeler in *42nd Street,* 1933.
Warner Brothers Pictures. Shorts and a sleeveless undershirt—standard
underwear over the decades.

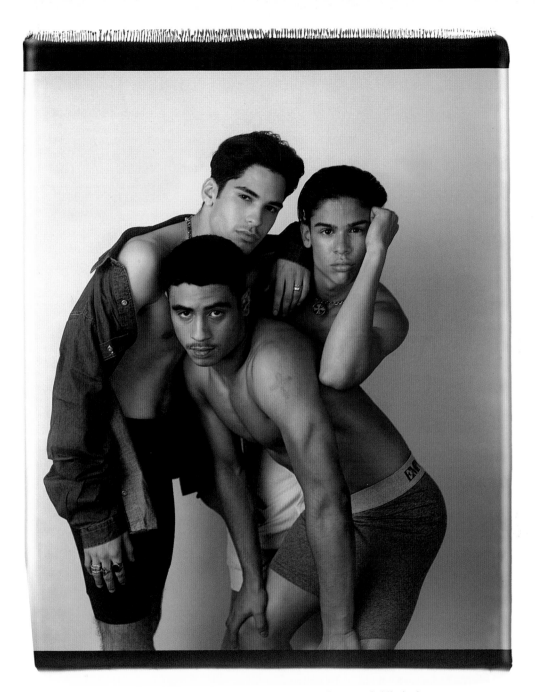

Tough underwear. *Above*, 1993. The music group Subliminal—
Michael Craig, Castro, and Richie Rivera—in an Emporio Armani
advertisement. Susan Shacter, American. Courtesy of the photographer. The
group seems an updated version of the tough guys in the painting opposite.

Opposite, PLAYGROUND, 1948, egg yolk tempera on masonite.
Paul Cadmus, American. Georgia Museum of Art, Athens, Georgia.
Underwear as outerwear is nothing new; what is new is that
wearing it in public now cuts across social lines.

The boxing game, 1988. *This page,* at Gleason's Gym, Brooklyn, New York. Actor Markus Flanagan, dressed in undershirt and black leggings, wearing a protective boxing cup.

Opposite, Fisher Stevens and Charlie Landry, of the Naked Angels Theater Company, posed in antique underwear. Susan Shacter, American. Both photographs courtesy of the photographer. Boxers have often been pictured in their underwear, starting in the era of John L. Sullivan.

Knits under all. *Above,* 1915. Kinosha Klosed Krotch Union Suits,
advertisement for the Cooper Underwear Company of Kenosha, Wisconsin.
J. C. Leyendecker, American. Union suits were so named, not because they
were union made, but because top and bottom were united on one piece.

Opposite, 1990. Men's knitted briefs by Jean Paul Gaultier. David Seidner,
American. Courtesy of the photographer. The suspenders are a nifty addition.

Waists away! *Opposite,* Lauritz Melchior, 1952. Alfred Eisenstaedt (1898–1995), German. Courtesy *Life* magazine. © Time Inc. The great Danish tenor in his dressing room at The Metropolitan Opera, strapped up for his 200th performance as Tristan.

Below, THE WHITE PAPER, 1958. Jean Cocteau (1886–1963), French. ©1996 ARS, New York/ADAGP/ Paris. The author's illustration shows part of the regulation underwear of the French sailor.

9

ABERRATION

Ab • er • ra • tion n. 1. A deviation from the proper or expected course.
2. A departure from the normal or typical.
3. A disorder or abnormal alteration in one's mental state.

The American Heritage Dictionary, Second College Edition

Is it an aberration when a woman wears her boyfriend's underwear? Suppose he wears hers? Cross-dressing, dressing in the garb or manner of the opposite sex, is usually viewed as an aberration when a man dresses as a woman. The reverse, women in men's clothes, is hardly thought about at all now that women wear pants as a matter of course. It was different in the times of Joan of Arc and George Sand. Saint Joan undoubtedly wore pants because how else could she function as a soldier? With George Sand, and later Marlene Dietrich, there was an interesting undercurrent of sexual ambiguity; whereas Katharine Hepburn in her slacks was more the American tomboy.

As opposed to drag queens, with their element of parody and specifically homosexual connotation, men who cross-dress in women's clothes play it straight and without exaggeration and are usually, when not indulging their fantasies, outwardly conservative members of society. Perhaps they're simply tired of boring men's suits and underthings, which have changed relatively little in the last two centuries. Female fashions, on the other hand—hemlines, necklines, silhouettes, and most of all, underpinnings—have been in a constant state of flux. As actor-director and sometime cross-dresser Charles Busch put it: "A boy has a thousand years of feminine excess from which to derive inspiration."

Andy Warhol and his Factory brought it all into the open in the late 1960s and 1970s with movies starring cross-dressers. Now, with ever more open discussion of sexual differences, drag queens have gone public. Ru Paul and others turn up on fashion runways where their appearance can be more exciting than the clothes. Lucky Cheng's, a restaurant in New York City's East Village (patronized, we are told, by such entertainment and international celebrities as Prince Albert of Monaco, Barbra Streisand, Bernadette Peters, and Al Pacino), has a waitstaff of drag queens wearing what might have led to an arrest in another era: bras, corsets, garter belts, the works. Then there's a school for "Boys Who Want to Be Girls" in lower Manhattan—the brainchild of Veronica Vera, an ex-star of pornographic movies—where the curriculum includes instruction in makeup, wig wearing, and the selection of both under- and outerwear. The graduation ceremony is a night on the town, dressed to kill. Tuition for a weekend is steep, but there is no shortage of students.

Frontispiece design for *The Full and True Account of The Wonderful Mission of Earl Lavender,* by John Davidson, 1895. Aubrey Beardsley (1872–1898), English. Private collection. A sadomasochistic fantasy with the illustrator's characteristic combination of eroticism and fetishism, both participants falling out of their underwear.

Sadomasochism is explicity tied to pain. Its wardrobe is filled with fetishistic elements, underwear translated into leather bras, metal-studded jockstraps, thong panties, and more. In sadomasochistic behavior, these become identifying garb. Provocative costumes accompany the whips, chains, and other pain-inducing paraphernalia of this subculture, a full range of which is available from catalogs and sex shops. Certainly tight-lacing has its sadomasochistic implications, implications fully realized by S&M's practitioners.

Were the college panty raids of the 1950s and 1960s a form of fetishism (imbuing an object with life, granting it a form of magic, or transferring to it some special power)? Perhaps it is attaching too much importance to them to say that the captured underpants were considered more than trophies, but why not? A German psychology book of 1913 devotes a chapter to "panty sniffing." Male interest in female underpants is obviously not a recent development.

As for "pornography," the ancient Greeks gave us the word, so the representation of sexually explicit behavior with the intention of causing sexual excitement is hardly a recent phenomenon. From soft porn like *Playboy* to the gritty hard-core variety, magazines picture women in suggestive or more explicit situations, either nude, or more likely, wearing some lingerie fragment. That the partially clad body is more exciting sexually than the naked is hardly news; a magazine columnist assigned to a story about a notorious nightclub of the 1970s told me that with all the nudity and sexual license confronting him, one woman wearing underwear seemed the most provocative person in the place. Hugh Hefner cap-

italized on the effect in his Playboy Clubs, where the waitress "bunnies" wore merry widow corsets so designed that the wearers couldn't lean over without their breasts spilling out and had to execute a neat plié to place drinks on the table.

So if none of this is new, what is? Probably it's the blurring of the line between what is acceptable in public discourse and what is not. From television, where once-banned brassiere ads are now accepted and any subject is open to discussion, to magazines and newspapers, to the even more public venue of bus shelters and billboards, underwear advertisements, both men's and women's, are ubiquitous and ever more explicit. Where does frankness end and aberration begin?

Drag queens, pornography, cross-dressing, sadomasochism, fetishism—by most definitions these kinkier manifestations of human sexuality would qualify as aberrations. Is it a coincidence that they all share a close association with underwear, women's underwear? Psychologists tell us that uncomfortable or painful clothing is tied to sexual arousal, so it's hardly surprising that women's underwear, so supremely uncomfortable for much of fashion history, has been a fertile source for men who dress up as women. That women over the centuries have endured tight lacing has no doubt enhanced their awareness of their bodies, but it does give pause that there are men similarly willing to truss themselves into the mini–torture chambers we call girdles, corsets, and waist cinchers. Is it the pain factor? Perhaps. Because, according to Havelock Ellis, "pain, itself, may...become an erotic symbol," and women's underclothes over the centuries have been rich in painful opportunity. ∎

The mesh-enhanced leg, 1959. Fernand Fonssagrives,
American. Courtesy of the photographer.
These precursors of today's panty hose would have been
worn only on stage or for purposes of seduction.

The universal attraction of black lace. *Opposite,* Carlo Mollino (1905–1973), Italian. © 1968 Carlo Mollino. Courtesy Robert Miller Gallery, New York City. Photograph by the architect-designer, one in a series of women in lingerie.

Below, WHAT'S FOR SALE: BLACK TEDDY, 1987, pencil and colored pencil on linen-backed paper on sculpted foam board. Larry Rivers, American. Courtesy of the artist.

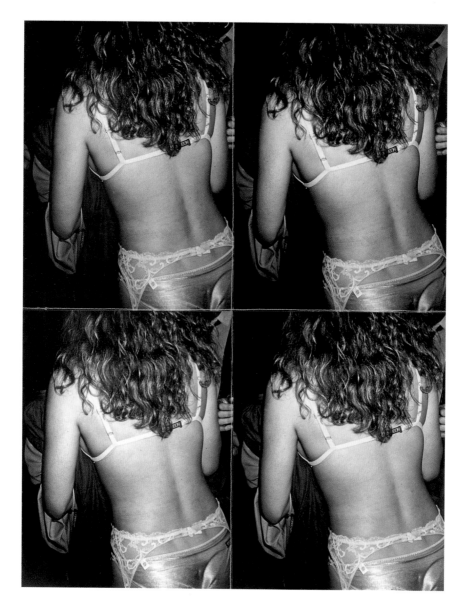

Satin underground. *Above,* 1976–86. Four prints sewn together with thread to make a single picture. Andy Warhol (1928–1987), American. © 1996 Andy Warhol Foundation for the Visual Arts/ARS, New York. Courtesy Robert Miller Gallery, New York City. Bra, garter belt, panties—one woman's underwear choices.

Opposite, 1988. Silano, American, for *Harper's Bazaar.* Courtesy of the photographer. Panties with a hint of boxer shorts and a very brief teddy.

Of human bondage. *This page*, Paris, 1929. Man Ray (1890–1976), American. A privately commissioned photograph. © 1996 ARS, New York/ADAGP/Man Ray Trust, Paris.

Opposite, New York, *ca.* 1950. Private collection. Fetishistic para-phernalia, intrinsic elements of sadomasochistic fantasy.

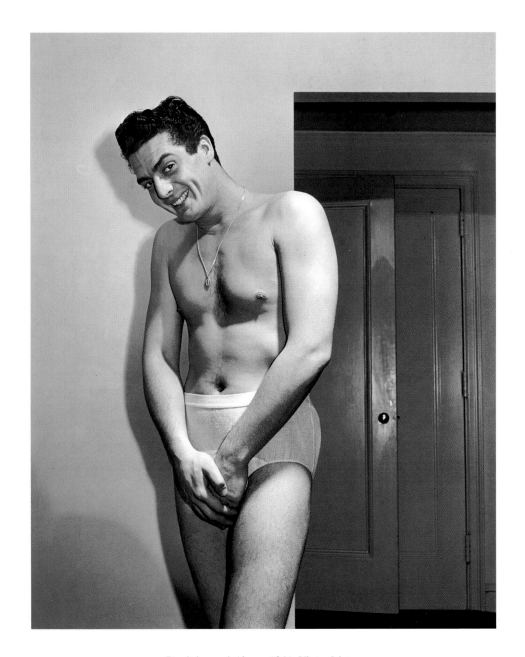

Don't be coy! *Above,* 1941. Victor Mature.
Alfred Eisenstaedt (1898–1995), German. Courtesy
Life magazine. © Time, Inc. The screen star as an
early underwear model.

Opposite, CINESIAS SOLICITING MYRRHINA,
1896, pen and ink. Aubrey Beardsley (1872–1898),
English: Drawing for Aristophanes' *Lysistrata,*
printed privately, 1896. The woman pursued wears
black stockings, and little else.

What went under the corset and long skirts? 1890.
English. Robert Dennis Collection, Miriam and Ira D.
Wallach Division of Art, Prints and Photographs,
The New York Public Library, Astor, Lenox and
Tilden Foundations. Each picture has a voyeur—in the
prudish Victorian era, the sight of women in their
underwear was very titillating.

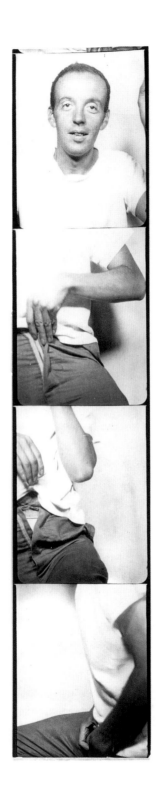

Private views. *Above,* 1995. New York rooftop. Duane Michals,
American. Courtesy of the photographer.

Opposite, ca. 1966. Taylor Mead, in an automatic photo booth,
doing a male strip. © 1996 Andy Warhol Foundation for the
Visual Arts/ARS, New York. Courtesy Robert Miller Gallery, New
York City. Andy Warhol routinely took people to Times Square
photo booths, then incorporated the pictures in his later work.

Cross-dressing. *Left,* TRYING ON MY BROTHER'S BREECHES, 1796, caricature. Richard Newton, English. The idea would have been very daring in an age when pants were strictly masculine apparel.

Opposite, ca. 1930. A classic comedy situation from an unidentified movie short; a man wearing women's underthings always gets a laugh.

The cross-dresser. R. F., 1916, France. Courtesy Janet Lehr, Inc., New York City. Taken over a period of years and carefully preserved in several albums, the photographs show the same unidentified man dressed in women's clothes, primarily underwear. Most probably R. F. took the pictures himself.

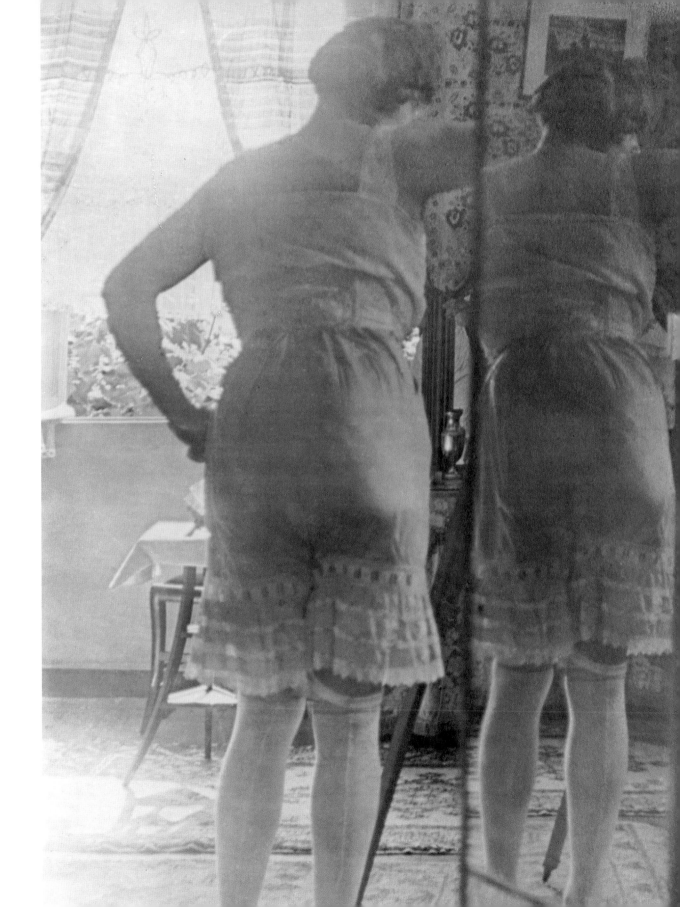

Underwear: different perspectives. *Opposite*, 1968. Surrealism at the service of fashion. Silano, American, for *Harper's Bazaar*. Courtesy of the photographer. Models in bra-slips, posed outdoors to appear as objects in space.

Below, WOMAN ON HER KNEES AND ELBOWS, 1914, gouache and black crayon on paper. Egon Schiele (1890–1918), Austrian. Private collection. Courtesy Galerie St. Etienne, New York City. Schiele frequently portrayed semidressed subjects, in this case wearing a petticoat and stockings gartered above the knee.

FREEDOM

I really do not see how it is possible for tight-lacers
to enter the kingdom of heaven.
Can suicides and infanticides be Christians?

Orson Fowler, nineteenth-century American writer

Surveying the history of underwear from our liberated vantage point we discover that, dissenters notwithstanding, from time immemorial, there's been a tendency to alter or distort the human body, and some form of compressing the waist and rib cage has been its most prominent feature. From Hippocrates to the English Puritans of the sixteenth and seventeenth centuries to some nineteenth-century Americans, physicians and moralists have inveighed against the corset. The Puritans called corsets the work of the devil, intended to transform women into unnatural creatures and to seduce men; Jean-Jacques Rousseau saw them as a corrupting device; Napoleon called them *"L'assassin de la race."* (Josephine is said to have owned 993 chemises but no mention is made of corsets.) *The Times* (London) stated that "tight lacing creates more domestic unhappiness than any other domestic circumstance in life."

Despite these attacks, whenever fashion deemed the corset necessary to mold the body to a current favored configuration, women wore it, and the wasp waist remained an emblem of elegance for centuries. There were periods of liberation such as that following the French Revolution, when there was also a revolt against corsets, hoops, petticoats, high-heeled shoes, and constricting children's clothes; even the practice of swathing infants' bodies was stopped. While these changes were undoubtedly healthful most were due more to fashion than to good sense. Women during the Directoire period were known to dampen their muslin gowns to make them cling so as to resemble the drapery of antique statues, hardly a healthful practice in the chilly damp of Parisian winters, and one causing serious outbreaks of bronchitis and pneumonia.

The march toward a liberated body proceeded in fits and starts—each step forward seemed to demand two steps back—and by the middle of the nineteenth century tight lacing was again the sine qua non of fashion. One would have expected the movement toward women's emancipation, which began midcentury in both the United States and England, to have made dress reform an issue, but while this was a concern, it did not have priority over women's suffrage. Indeed, during the height of the demonstrations before World War I, in fact, the suffragettes marched, picketed, and were duly arrested wearing the customary costumes of their day, complete with corsets and elabo-

ISADORA DUNCAN AT THE PORTAL OF THE PARTHENON, 1921. Edward Steichen (1879–1973), American, for *Vanity Fair* magazine. The Museum of Modern Art, New York City, gift of the photographer. Duncan, pioneer of modern dance, based her life and art on the Greek ideal of the liberated body. Her costume, an interpretation of the antique Greek tunic, was worn over little or nothing at all.

rate hats. Perhaps they deplored any concern with fashion, either for or against, as frivolity. The cause of freedom for women made little headway until shortly before the war; then, as women began to loosen their stays and step out of their multiple petticoats, war hastened the process, leading to the all-encompassing liberation of the 1920s.

Earlier in the nineteenth century, repeated attempts were made to give women more mobility by dressing them in trouser-bottomed costumes. In the Oneida Community in central New York, pantaloons were worn during the 1860s, and women in the Klondike wore them in the 1890s as a practical matter. Midcentury, a cousin of the suffragist Elizabeth Cady Stanton devised a costume modeled on a Turkish woman's outfit, consisting of a gathered pantaloon bottom and a tunic overblouse. It was publicized and adopted by Amelia Bloomer, a well-known feminist writer and editor, hence the name "bloomers," and was worn by a few brave women here and abroad. Reviled and derided, bloomers never really caught on; they conflicted with the strong prejudice against women wearing what were considered masculine garments: Pants-wearing women might come to dominate their husbands. According to a cartoon in the British magazine *Punch:* "As the husband, shall the wife be; he will have to wear a gown if he does not quickly make her put her Bloomer short-coats down." Eventually, the name came to be used to describe any sort of gathered, bifurcated garment, usually underpants. Again, at the beginning of the twentieth century, French fashion designer Paul Poiret led the way toward the acceptance of trousers for women when he introduced "Orientalist" fashion, a "lampshade tunic" worn over trousers, thereby once more "liberating Western women from the tyranny of the corset." It was too extreme for street wear but the fashion caught on, and for a while, lounging pajamas became all the rage.

As for children, in this country both boys and girls of the nineteenth century wore skirts as infants. Girls as young as five were put in stays and even little boys in their frocks were braced by whalebone and buckram. At the age of six or seven, both began to be dressed similarly to their parents. According to a New York Historical Society account, "Upper-class clothing was uncomfortable for both sexes. Happily, less than 3 percent of the population was of such exalted rank that they had to submit to these European fashions. Lower-class children wore plainer, more comfortable clothing."

What finally brought about the liberation of the body? Women's participation in sports, the introduction of the bicycle and then the automobile, World War I, winning the vote, health concerns, and, yes, technology—each of these has had an effect; together they've made possible forward strides that, at last, don't require two steps back. If women, or men for that matter, decide to put on girdles or waist cinchers or push-up bras, it's not a question of conformity, it's a matter of choice, another diversion in the stream of fashion that goes back to our earliest ancestors. So let's not judge; let's just sit back and enjoy the spectacle. ■

Backstage. 1956. PARIS STRIP-
TEASEUSES. Frank Horvat, French.
Courtesy Staley-Wise Gallery, New York
City. Stripped down to the basic brief.

SELECTED BIBLIOGRAPHY

The following bibliography includes only a selection of the many books in which John Esten and I found information relative to the subject of the history of underwear. In addition, there were forays into the stacks and closets and reading rooms of a number of museum costume collections, plus encyclopedias, periodicals, and newspaper clippings. We received anecdotal material from friends and even generous strangers who heard about the project. The research led to sources that may seem far afield, such as looking into the history of indoor plumbing, or an Encyclopedia of Christian Thought. Some odd material was found in Annie Sprinkle's *Post Modern Pinups*, coauthored by Veronica Vera, headmistress of the School for Boys Who Want to Be Girls. There is no telling where such research can lead. In the twenty-odd years in which this book has been an on-again, off-again hobby project in the making, it has taken me down curious paths and led to offbeat dinner-party conversations. I learned that the few so-called "experts" often disagree about when a given item of underwear was conceived, or whether people slept in the nude in a given period. The guesswork and sleuthing have been as much fun as the source-checking. I hope and trust that we have contributed something new to the subject.

Armitage, Shirley. *Illustrator of the Jazz Age, John Held, Jr.* Syracuse, NY: Syracuse University Press, 1987.

Beaton, Cecil. *The Glass of Fashion.* London: Shenval Press, Ltd., 1954.

Beerbohm, Max. *Seven Men.* New York: Alfred A. Knopf, 1920.

Blum, Daniel. *A Pictorial History of the American Theatre, 1860–1976.* New York: Crown, 1977.

——. *A Pictorial History of the Talkies.* New York: G.P. Putnam's Sons, 1958.

Brill, Dianne. *Boobs, Boys and High Heels.* New York: Penguin Books, 1992.

Contini, Mila. *Fashion from Ancient Greece to the Present Day.* New York: Odyssey Press, 1965.

Davis, John Langdon. "Lady Godiva, the Future of Nakedness." *Harper's* magazine, 1928.

Darrah, William C. *World of Stereographs.* Gettysburg, PA: W. C. Darrah, 1977.

DePauw, Linda, and Conover Hunt. *Women in America.* New York: Viking Press, 1978.

Dictionary of the History of Ideas. New York: Charles Scribner's Sons, 1954.

Ewing, Elizabeth. *Dress and Undress.* New York: Charles Scribner's Sons, 1978.

Esten, John. *Man Ray: Bazaar Years.* New York: Rizzoli International Publications, 1985.

Fisher, Angela. *Africa Adorned.* New York: Harry N. Abrams, Inc., 1984.

Fuchs, Eduard. *Die Frau in der Karikatur.* Munich: Albert Langen, 1907.

Garland, Madge. *The Changing Face of Beauty.* New York: M. Barrows & Company, 1957.

Guerinet, Armand. *Le Coustume chez les Peuples Anciens et Modernes.* Paris: F. Hottenroth, Editions Rene Budin (no date).

Hiler, Hilaire. *From Nudity to Raiment.* New York: Weyhe, 1929.

Hollander, Anne. *Seeing Through Clothes*. New York: Alfred A. Knopf, 1978.

——. *Sex and Suits*. New York: Alfred A. Knopf, 1994.

Hawthorne, Rosemary. *Knickers*. London: Souvenir Press, 1985.

——. *Bras*. London: Souvenir Press, 1992.

Kallir, Jane. *Egon Schiele: The Complete Works*. New York: Harry Abrams, 1990.

Keenan, Brigid. *Dior in Vogue*. New York: Harmony Books, 1981.

Kunhardt, Philip B., Jr. *Life: The First 50 Years, 1936–1986*. Boston: Little, Brown, 1986.

Lafayette, Madame de. *La Princesse de Clèves*. Paris: Editions Nilsson, 1957.

Laver, James. *The Concise History of Costume and Fashion*. England: Thames and Hudson, 1969.

MacKenzie, Midge. *Shoulder to Shoulder*. New York: Alfred A. Knopf, 1975.

Martin, Richard, and Harold Koda. *Infra-Apparel*. New York: The Metropolitan Museum of Art, 1993.

Moffitt, Peggy, and William Claxton. *The Rudi Gernreich Book*. New York: Rizzoli International Books, 1991.

Morel, Juliette. *Lingerie Parisienne*. London: Academy Editions, 1976.

Rudofsky, Bernard. *Are Clothes Modern?* New York: Paul Thiebold, 1947.

——. *The Unfashionable Human Body*. New York: Paul Thiebold, 1971.

St. Laurent, Cecil. *A History of Women's Underwear*. New York: Rizzoli International Press, 1966.

——. *The Great Book of Lingerie*. New York: The Vendome Press, 1986.

Stegemeyer, Anne. *Who's Who in Fashion*. New York: Fairchild Publications, 1996.

Tice, Bill. *Enticements*. New York: Macmillan Publishing Company, 1985.

Waugh, Norah. *Corsets and Crinolines*. London: B.T. Batsford, Ltd., 1954.

Wharton, Edith. *A Backward Glance*. New York: Appleton-Century-Crofts, 1934.

Willet, C., and P. Cunnington. *The History of Underclothes*. London: Michael Joseph (no date).

WASP WAIST, 1994, serigraph. Kurt Vonnegut, American writer-artist. Courtesy of the artist. This exaggerated view of the female body is consistent with Vonnegut's famously offbeat sensibility.

LAUNDRY, PORTUGAL, 1994.
Zoe Leonard, American.
Courtesy Paula Cooper Gallery,
New York City. Inevitably,
"It all comes out in the wash."

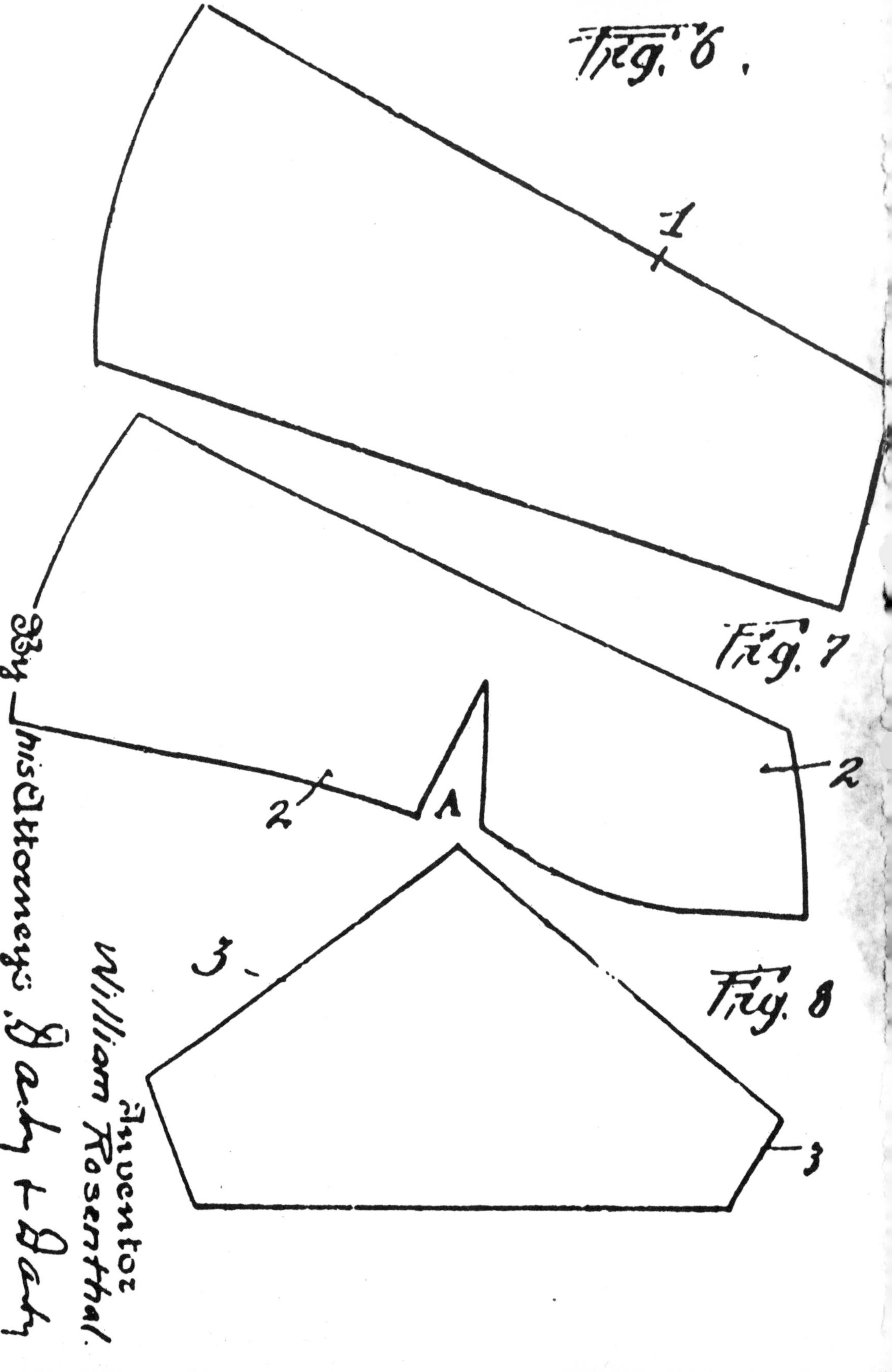

Fig. 6.

1

Fig. 7

2

A

2

Fig. 8

3

3

By his Attorneys:

William Rosenthal.

Inventor

Baldy & Baldy